Assuring Quality for the
Social Studies in Our Schools

Education and Society

Paul R. Hanna and Gerald A. Dorfman, series editors

Publications in the Education and Society series, a research project of the Hoover Institution on War, Revolution and Peace, address issues of education's role in social, economic, and political affairs. It is hoped that insight into the relationship between inculcated values and behavior and a society's approach to development will contribute to more effective education for the establishment and preservation of justice, freedom, and peace.

Unconditional Democracy: Education and Politics in Occupied Japan, 1945–1952
Toshio Nishi

Education and Social Change in China: The Beginnings of the Modern Era
Sally Borthwick

Educational Reform and Administrative Development: The Cases of Colombia and Venezuela
E. Mark Hanson

Assuring Quality for the Social Studies in Our Schools
Paul R. Hanna

ASSURING QUALITY FOR THE SOCIAL STUDIES IN OUR SCHOOLS

Paul R. Hanna

SENIOR RESEARCH FELLOW
HOOVER INSTITUTION ON WAR, REVOLUTION AND PEACE

LEE L. JACKS PROFESSOR EMERITUS
SCHOOL OF EDUCATION, STANFORD UNIVERSITY

HOOVER INSTITUTION PRESS

STANFORD UNIVERSITY   STANFORD, CALIFORNIA

Hoover Press Publication 350

First printing, 1987

Manufactured in the United States of America

92 91 90 89 88 87   9 8 7 6 5 4 3 2 1

Library of Congress Cataloging in Publication Data

Hanna, Paul Robert, 1902–
    Assuring quality for the social studies in our
schools.

    (Education and society)
    1. Social sciences—Study and teaching (Elementary)—United States—Curricula.   2. Social sciences—Study and teaching (Secondary)—United States—Curricula.
3. Social sciences—Study and teaching—United States—Evaluation.   4. Education—United States—Aims and objectives.   I. Title.   II. Series.
LB1584.H279   1987   372.8'3043   86-34278
ISBN 0-8179-8502-6

Design by P. Kelley Baker

CONTENTS

FOREWORD

In this slender volume, we have further proof that Paul Hanna's old ideas can be timelier and more interesting than almost anyone else's newest notions. But we also have, even if the author did not intend it, an implicit commentary on much that has changed in the institutions and attitudes of American education during the nearly three decades since he floated the idea of building a consensus on a national curriculum.

One need not agree, then or now, with Paul's specific curricular preferences in order to share his perception of the critical underlying issues. I, for example, have never favored the "expanding communities" approach to social studies, an approach Paul Hanna had much to do with developing. But I much admire his keen awareness that curricular content—what children actually study in school—matters hugely, and that the decisions we make in this domain must depend on our answers to the single most important question that can be asked about education: what exactly is it that we want the next generation to know when it leaves school?

Most of the recent reports on school reform that catalyzed today's "excellence movement" stop short of answering that fundamental question. They settle instead for prescribing a certain number—usually a larger number—of years, courses, or credits that a young person must earn in various subjects before graduating from high school. In effect, the reformers have urged that more notches be carved in the youngster's pencil, more scalps nailed to his transcript, more days and hours spent in the learning process. And I agree. But to prescribe four years of English or three years of math is the easy part. The challenge, the truly important part, is to specify what children shall learn during these years. Yet few contemporary educational reformers, at least at the national level, have attempted to do so.

One can get in deep trouble nowadays by talking about anything that smacks of a "national curriculum," and as I read Paul's collection it became plain that the danger was no less a quarter-century ago. Yet in one sense the issue is even more pressing now than then; for while Paul did not use today's fashionable term, "cultural literacy," his essays are suffused with that concern. What is it, he asks, that all young Americans need to know if they are truly to become members of the same adult society, heirs to a shared culture, transmitters of a common heritage—one that changes with each generation as it is influenced by immigrant newcomers who, even as they become a part of it, alter it forever. During the years since Paul penned these essays we have, as Stephen Thernstrom has written, become so preoccupied with the *pluribus* in our national motto that we have paid too little attention, especially in our school curriculum, to the *unum*.

Hence this collection speaks to our time, and not only as a memento of the period in which the essays and lectures were first prepared. The issues Paul raises are ours; the questions he poses are questions we still need to answer.

In his most fully developed proposal regarding a possible national curriculum, Paul recommended that a nongovernmental commission be formed to conduct the study. He was right then about the desirability of keeping such a body separate from the national government; the same caution is still warranted. The last thing the United States needs is a federal curriculum prescription. But we have gotten better in recent years— at least, some of us hope we have—at distinguishing between educational issues of national significance and those that should be addressed directly by the federal government. A decade back, readers would likely have been perplexed by Paul's suggestion. How, they would have asked, can a national commission be separate and distinct from the federal government? Today, I think, this is easier to visualize. Indeed, one can easily imagine a commission—not so different from the National Commission on Excellence in Education—impaneled by the federal government, possibly even paid for by the federal taxpayer, whose recommendations would consist not of a laundry list of new programs or regulations for Washington to promulgate but of a set of prescriptions aimed at those who really matter in American education: parents, teachers, principals, community leaders, local and state policymakers, taxpayers, and voters.

No longer do we assume that Uncle Sam must solve every problem he calls attention to. In the field of education, increasingly, we know that he ought not.

Yet there remains merit in Paul's proposal that an examination of the national goals of education be undertaken completely outside the federal orbit. What does not ring as true today—it is perhaps the only part of the volume that does not—is the suggestion that the National Education Association is the proper sponsor for such a study. How many among us would willingly consign to today's NEA the most important decisions about what our children should learn in school? To paraphrase Mr. Buckley, I would sooner entrust those choices to the collective wisdom of the first hundred persons in the phone book or, if the truth be told, to the first hundred members of the NEA itself. One of the things that makes life bearable in 1986 is the awareness that most of that union's individual members share few of the obdurate political views of their national organization.

But my purpose here is not to criticize the NEA. It is merely to suggest that were we to carry out Paul Hanna's vision today, we would have to find another aegis for the national commission he suggests.

Could we find one? Truth to tell, I'm not confident that we could; not confident that the public would trust any existing organization of educators or that the educators would trust each other. One might wish for a new Carnegie Commission, or for the sponsorship of another major foundation. But of late they seem more interested in social and political activism than in educational quality.

Perhaps, at least for now, we should refocus our sights for curriculum renovation on the level that plainly can undertake a searching scrutiny of the problem and, better still, can do something with the results. I refer, of course, to the states, several of which have recently commenced just such inquiries, enveloping curricular objectives, issues of scope and sequence, even textbook appraisals. None is more impressive to me than the program currently underway in California, so ably led by Bill Honig. Perhaps other states can do the same; perhaps they will prefer to see what California comes up with.

I have half a hunch that Paul may agree. In the 1950s and 1960s states were not the sources of educational reform and innovation that they are today. It was more common then to think of changes in education as inevitably and properly national. Perhaps Paul will bear with the suggestion that these days we can look to the states for serious leadership in curricular matters as in so many other educational policy issues.

One thing I so admire about Paul Hanna is that if he doesn't agree with my previous statements—or, for that matter, with anything else—I can be confident that he will tell me so. Indeed, he might give an address or write an article or even another book to explain his views. But I also know that whatever is said or written will be presented with that rare blend of humility and confidence, kindliness and certitude, that characterizes Paul's works as well as his person.

Paul Hanna continues to make immense contributions to education in the United States and around the world, as he has throughout a lifespan that is nearly twice my own. His scholarship, erudition, unflagging energy, and deep reserves of concern and compassion are the stuff of legends. His freshness of vision is as laudable today as it ever was. The archive that he is working tirelessly to assemble at the Hoover Institution—fittingly named for Paul and his wife Jean—already bids fair to be the most important education archive in the land. I salute and thank him, even as I commend to others the interesting, timely, and thought-inducing volume that follows.

CHESTER E. FINN, JR.
Assistant Secretary,
U.S. Department of Education

INTRODUCTION

The curricula of our elementary and secondary schools are under nationwide attack. Discussion regarding reform is widespread.

In 1957, I published an article suggesting a model social studies curriculum for the schools. The response to that article stimulated me to think further about how we could provide a civic education for our children and youth that would expose them to our most basic values and concepts and develop the abilities necessary for the survival and progress of our democratic society. During the following years, as I learned more, I spoke and wrote frequently on the subject. The eight reprints that follow mirror the evolution of my thinking as I received both criticism and support for my proposed procedures for accomplishing my goals.

Since 1957, national concern for the improvement of civic education has waxed and waned, but little action has resulted. Today the public is deeply aware of the need to strengthen our civic education as well as education in the humanities, mathematics, and science. We have had a flood of commission reports on what is wrong and how we might move to regain excellence in our schools.

Some of those who recall the suggestions I made a quarter of a century ago have urged that the earlier discussion be made available for a new generation of readers. Thus the rationale for producing this set of reprints.

EDITOR'S NOTE: These articles have been previously published. Other than corrections of spelling and the renumbering of some footnotes, the originals have been faithfully reproduced.

Assuring Quality for the Social Studies in Our Schools

At the time this article was written I had been seeking for several years to formu-late an acceptable scope and sequence for a series of social studies textbooks I was preparing. A booklet entitled The Future of the Social Studies, *edited by James A. Michener for the National Council for the Social Studies, stimulated me to try my hand at sketching and publishing a framework.*

This paper, originally delivered as a lecture at Syracuse University in 1957, sketches a proposed scope-and-sequence curriculum in social studies. Although this first reprint may be longer than some readers will have the interest or time to pursue, it will provide an understanding of the framework of my ideas regarding a civic education curriculum for the elementary and middle school years.

SOCIETY—CHILD—CURRICULUM*

1

Roughly ten thousand years ago, man began to play a role in that phase of our earth's story which we now call civilization. The story of society, of the child, and of society's efforts to educate the child is as old as civilization itself.

For as far back in human history as we can go, we find man striving to pass on his understanding of his world to his children. Every society known to us through written records or anthropological investigation has attempted to explain to its young how the earth was made, how man came to inhabit the earth, how man assembled his kind into communities, and how man has developed tools, laws, and institutions to guarantee the good life for that community.

Each society has some plan for passing on its social heritage through instruction and initiation. Before writing was invented, much of this instruction was passed from generation to generation through the telling of tales. Later, when man could record his thoughts in writing, the elders wrote the story of earth and of man so that their works would sustain the cherished ways of society and protect the faiths of the fathers.

Consider, for instance, how Moses spoke to the elders of Israel as he prepared his people to flee Egypt: "And it shall come to pass when your

*From *Education 2000 AD*, edited by Clarence W. Hunnicutt. Syracuse, N.Y.: Syracuse University Press, 1956. Reprinted by permission of the publisher.

children shall say unto you, what mean ye by this service?"[1] Then the fathers were to tell anew the old tales and explain to a younger generation the ways of their society.

To speak of the Bible reminds us that the history of child education in America, in turn, is as old as the first settlers who sought to mold their children into the special type of adult needed in colonial communities. The children of the pilgrim and the pioneer used the Bible as a text as they learned the ways of their society by interacting with adults of the family and of the immediate community. These adults sought to pass on to their young the ways of behaving that insured survival and progress in a new and rugged environment.

Today we can look back at our own American history and the story of all other societies as we know them and say with surety that every people in every time has sought to educate its children. This process of educating can be termed a basic human activity.

Let us now make a leap in time and concern ourselves with the **changing** conceptions of society, the child and the curriculum as we have known them during the half century that the School of Education of Syracuse University has grown and flourished.

In order to cover this half century quickly so that we may concentrate on the assignment that faces us today, will you consider two sharply drawn caricatures of the relationships between society, the child, and the curriculum?

These two pictures are sketched in the most general of terms and separated by the most arbitrary of dates. I present them only to insure that you understand the general frame of reference within which we will work.

At the close of the last century the needs of society were served by educationally transmitting the social heritage so that [a stable] society might be maintained from one generation to the next. The curriculum was viewed as a collection of subject-matter courses organized in a manner thought to facilitate memorization of the content. The child was considered to be a receptacle into which knowledge could be poured. In such an educational frame of reference, the needs of society were supreme; the child's mind was a blank tablet on which the school was to write the wisdom of the ancestors by a process of verbalization and drill. The transmission of the social heritage was the sole concern of education.

During the first quarter of this century, educators came to view the needs of society differently. The improvement of society was emphasized more than transmission of knowledge; improvement was thought to be dependent on the creative effort of the individual. The curriculum evolved into unstructured activities initiated by wants and desires of pupils who were urged to express themselves freely. The child was considered to be a delicate flower unfolding its petals of interest to a world of endless activity. In such an educational climate the needs and nature of society were of secondary importance, child interest reigned supreme, and the ideal curriculum was whatever the child and teacher found most attractive.

Such pictures as these caricatures call to mind may make some of you uncomfortable as you remember many capable and conscientious teachers who never thought about the child as either a passive receptacle or an unfolding flower.

Some of you will remember that John Dewey, Francis Parker, and others placed emphasis on the child in the days when most schools stressed content memorization; many of you will recall that John Childs, Harold Rugg, and others placed emphasis on the nature of society in the days when many schools stressed the interests and growth patterns of childhood. But I have deliberately drawn these distinctions more sharply than is justified in order to impress you with the notion that the earlier emphasis in education was on the nature of society—and that the later emphasis is on the nature of the child.

Today, many educators wish to know why the curriculum should be dominated by either the child or the society. The needs of each are interrelated in such ways that the nature of society and the nature of childhood are indispensable to a balanced curriculum. On the one hand, the curriculum is based upon a regard for the individual child and his optimum growth as valuable ends in society. The individual child whose basic emotional needs are being met in ways acceptable to society is the "father of the self-respecting man" who can take his useful place in the activities of living and working for the common welfare of our society.

On the other hand, the curriculum imparts to the young that knowledge which perpetuates and enriches the society. We recognize three great strands of knowledge: the social sciences dealing with the man-to-man relationships; the humanities dealing with the man-to-spirit relationships; and the natural sciences dealing with the man-to-thing relationships. A full consideration of the topic "society, the child, and the curriculum" would necessarily develop equally each of these three strands of the curriculum framework. Because we are limited for time, we have selected for illustration only that strand most closely identified with society and the child—the social studies. We shall leave to others delineation of designs for the other two broad fields of the curriculum.

Let us examine the problem more closely. First, we will consider the selection of socially significant content. Then, we will review briefly the nature of the child and a few principles of learning. And finally, we will present an illustrative design for a balanced social studies program that is rooted both in the society and in the child.

Before we continue, however, I recognize that this topic needs a delicate touch; for there are still some who rise in alarm at the mention of content drawn from our social heritage and cry out that they do not wish a return to the curriculum of the last century. May we say that nobody who has studied with care the schools of a generation ago and compared them with schools of today would for a moment advocate a return to the exclusively "content-centered" curriculum of the past. But just as we seek no return to an earlier extreme, neither are we satisfied with dallying around the opposite polarity.

Society and the Problem of Content

What shall we select from our social heritage to form the solid core of citizenship training? What common understanding and behavior provide the cement which holds our society together?

Our heritage from society is, in all truth, a blend of yesterday and today. The atomic bomb is as much a part of our heritage as is the long-bowman of Lancashire; automation as much a part as is the spinning jenny; the NATO agreement as much as the Monroe Doctrine. One gives perspective to the other, and behind both the historical and contemporary are generalizations and values essential to obtaining ultimate peace and order in our world.

But the problem of selecting and organizing content from our historical and contemporary social heritage is no simple matter. You understand that as the scholars have focused their inquiry on one phase of man's activities after another, the range, volume, and complexity of what is understood grow steadily greater. Such extension of knowledge promises man an increasing control over his destiny and makes imperative the need for each citizen to know more than did his forefathers. In our capacity as guides of the learning process, educators cannot escape this personal responsibility to try to keep growing in wisdom as the dimensions of our knowledge expand.

A major difficulty faced by the school staff is that of selecting the most significant content from this expanding store of knowledge about the social, economic, and political behavior of men. Several efforts are currently being made to solve this difficult problem of selection. I want briefly to review four of them for you.

Some of you here may have heard of the efforts of the California State Central Committee on the Social Studies[2] to identify concepts from the social sciences for use in designing, in broad outlines, a curriculum for California schools. This is a cooperative effort by a state department of education, scholars in the social science disciplines, specialists in child development, and schoolmen and schoolwomen. Their efforts to blend the concepts of society and the nature of the child in designing a curricular framework for the social studies promises exciting results and could be of use in the school curriculum of states other than California.

Another investigation worthy of consideration was conducted by Malcolm Douglass[3] into the professional literature of geography. Douglass undertook to identify and classify the interrelationships persisting between man and his physical environment. This study, the most comprehensive and scholarly of its kind in some time, has been well received by both educators and geographers and has begun to have its impact on extending the geographic content of the elementary school curriculum.

A third example of selecting content for the social studies from a social science discipline can be illustrated in the recent six weeks Northwestern University School of Education workshop in geography led by Professors Clyde Kohn and Donald Hughes. Ten leading geographers presented papers to the workshop dealing with the geographic relationships of the United States since 1945. The workshop members were grouped into eight committees that extracted the geographic generalizations from these papers and discussed this content in terms of curriculum development and teaching methods. Under the guidance of the workshop leaders, these committees then wrote group papers dealing with these generalizations in terms of curricular scope and sequence. These papers were then added to the papers prepared by the geographers and the combined manuscripts will soon be published under the title *The U.S.A. in the Modern World.*[4]

A final illustration of such content research can be found in several current investigations by Stanford graduate students. These researchers are engaged in a cross-disciplinary study of the social science disciplines for the purposes of providing principals, teachers, and other curriculum makers with a synthesizing report of generalizations drawn from the literature of the social sciences. These generalizations can be used in the social studies strand of the curriculum in much the same way that the principles of natural science have been used in building science courses for the elementary school.

Let me caution you that the intent underlying these investigations mentioned is not to attempt the impossible. These researchers have no thought of making professional social science researchers out of elementary school youngsters. They consider that the logical order of arranging content found in the social sciences or the methods traditionally utilized by scholars to teach advanced university students are not—I repeat, **not**—appropriate for the immature youngsters of our elementary schools.

To anticipate the next section of this discussion, let me assure you that elementary teachers understand and utilize modern methods of guiding learning that are better suited to our pupils than those we could copy from collegiate instruction.

The Child and the Problem of Method

Like the man who came to dinner, bio-psychological studies created a furor in the early days of this century when the curriculum was dominated by textbooks best suited for maintaining the status quo. Fifty years of careful experimentation and accurate measurement, however, have made bio-psychological theory a welcome guest in the halls of education. Though many research efforts have advanced the methodology of teaching and improved the construction of curriculums, we can allot space to examine just one of the principles of psychology which we have tested in practice and from which we have developed dependable classroom methods.

You will recall that the older theories of learning thought of motivation as generated by the will. Any pupil supposedly could successfully master any school task if he would just work hard enough. "Put your shoulder to the wheel" and "keep your nose to the grindstone" were oft repeated phrases of that day—but most pupil motivation lay either in trying to get a gold star or in avoiding an application of the hickory stick.

Today all major schools of psychology contend that the pupil must be interested for effective learning to take place. Teachers have become committed to the idea that pupil interest must be aroused before pupil effort attends the lesson. The modern teacher, however, does not view child interest as something possessed by the child at birth. Interests are primarily the residue of one's prior experiences stimulated by current experience. What a pupil is exposed to over the TV set, in the comic book, at the family meal, in the streetcorner culture—these experiences shape the child's interests. Knowing these chance stimuli are both unselected and unevaluated, and that a better set of interests in the child would motivate more significant learnings, the school now deliberately decides what kinds of pupil interest are preferable and then sets a stage or creates an environment to arouse that interest. One of the school's greatest tasks is to stimulate and arouse pupil interest of the most worthy type.

Having created an interest-arousing environment, the teacher then uses the resulting interests and purposes to the limit to assure good teaching-learning.

There is little disagreement among us over the value of the contributions made by the bio-psychological sciences. We are often sharply critical of these foundation sciences for not giving us more and sounder cues for educational practice. There are, however, several principles that definitely have implications for properly designing a balanced curriculum. To review these: each segment of the curriculum must provide a wide range of possible educative experiences to fit a spread of maturation levels; within this spread, the curriculum must be flexible enough to permit adaptation to another range of individual differences so that each pupil can be provided with selected and evaluated educative experiences beginning where past experiences left off; the experiences must be such that they will arouse in the individual sound purposes in accord with the developmental tasks he seeks to accomplish; the experiences should be well organized in the sense that they flow from previous experiences and lead toward specific pupil-accepted goals so that the possibilities of transfer are enhanced.

The Theory of Curriculum Design

The assertion that the elementary school curriculum must be designed or organized rather than formless or haphazard is basic to any improvement in the curriculum. As the educator must understand the nature and needs of his society and survey the interests and capacities of his pupils, so John Dewey says he must also:

> arrange the conditions which provide the subject-matter or content for experiences that satisfy these needs and develop these capacities. The planning must be flexible enough to permit free play for individuality of experience and yet firm enough to give direction towards continuous development of power.[5]

When we speak of planning or designing the curriculum, we refer to a process that has at least two stages. Some aspects of the curriculum must be carefully planned in advance, while others are best planned just prior to or during the educative experiences.

First, what is designed in advance? The representatives of the people and their selected educational leaders decide what objectives best suit the educational purposes of the society. These objectives give direction to the efforts of the school staff as they work to make these objectives operational. The over-all curriculum pattern should then be drawn to include those understandings and behaviors which the school staff believe are required for competent citizenship in the several communities of men, and should be drawn in harmony with that staff's knowledge about the nature of childhood. In advance, the school faculty not only design the over-all scope and sequence of learning experiences for all grades, but they sketch in the broad but flexible framework for each grade. Attention here is given to the maturation characteristics of children as cues to the understandings and behaviors that can be developed at various grade levels.

Second, what is designed in process? Teacher-pupil planning is a joint enterprise that cannot be structured in advance. Any sound educational experience depends upon the interaction of the learner and his environment. The unique personality of each pupil and each class vitally influence the immediate choice of activity. The unpredicted happenings of the kaleidoscopic events of the day are often the stimuli that spark pupil interest which the teacher can put to good use in guiding the teaching-learning experiences toward the desired objectives. These individual pupil differences and the stimulating events of a changing life can only affect the curriculum planning while the educative experiences are underway. The teacher, always the most important member of the class group, guides the pupils in designing in process within the broad, flexible framework of that which was designed by the school staff in advance.

Objectives: The First Step

A single course of study or the standardization of learning experiences for all American schools is out of the question. But because all Americans hold in common certain objectives for education, and because school faculties judge certain behavior to be more desirable than other behaviors, we are charged with the responsibility of providing an over-all curriculum framework incorporating these objectives and leading to experiences within which children may develop these behaviors.

One of the most difficult problems of curriculum construction, however, involves the translation of these educational objectives into educative experiences. Once a school staff has worked with its community in determining the general objectives for education in that community, then the staff must have accepted the responsibility of stating these objectives in behavorial terms. After this, the staff must provide itself with a curricular framework within which pupil experiences may lead to achievement of these objectives. In order to build such a framework, the school staff must next concern itself with those elements of design that we term **scope** and **sequence**.

Scope: The Second Step

Scope refers to the breadth and depth of content and experiences to be provided within the social studies program. The scope can be thought of as the **what** of the curriculum.

CHART 1
CATEGORIES OF BASIC HUMAN ACTIVITIES:
THE WHEEL OF LIFE

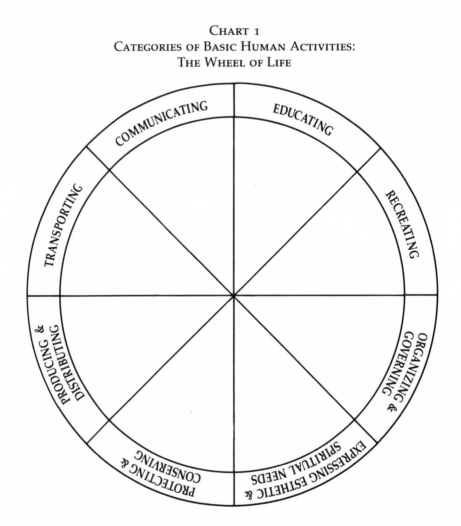

For our purposes, the scope or range of content can be grouped in eight categories of basic human activities that represent the efforts of men to meet their needs in a social setting and to solve their problems arising from man-to-man relationships. These eight categories of activities are illustrated in Chart 1 as a wheel divided into eight wedges. Such a catalog of basic human activities, universally carried on by all societies regardless of time or location, is now widely used in our American elementary schools.

This particular way of organizing the scope of the social studies program has been found to have several advantages over other, less carefully planned designs: first, the eight categories make up the totality of the citizenship activities in which all Americans need to develop competence; second, the list can be used as a checklist against which the teacher and pupils test the comprehensiveness of what is planned in process; third, such a list suggests content drawn both from the ongoing life of the pupils and from the literature of the social sciences.

Sequence: The Third Step

Sequence refers to the continuity and order of experiences provided from year to year throughout the pupil's school career. The sequence can be thought of as the **when** of the curriculum.

The sequence of themes or emphases for the social studies program of the elementary school should not be determined solely either by child nature or by the inner logic of content. But combining the nature and demands of the child and the nature and demands of society, it is possible to arrive at a logically and a psychologically defensible curriculum design.

For our purposes, the sequence of emphases can be sketched in eleven expanding and concentric communities of men. These concentric communities are illustrated in Chart 2.

The world of the child obviously represents the widening horizons which he experiences as he grows up. The world for the baby is the area surrounding his crib and the population of that world is his family. Later, his world becomes the family house and yard, and the population of this world is the family and all who service and visit the home. Still later, the world becomes the urban block or the rural township in which the home is located; its population naturally increases to include the neighbors. After the child bursts the bounds of the block or the township, his world begins to expand rapidly as he comes into contact with more people living in larger and larger arenas.

CHART 2
EXPANDING COMMUNITIES OF MEN:
EMPHASIS FOR GRADE ALLOCATION

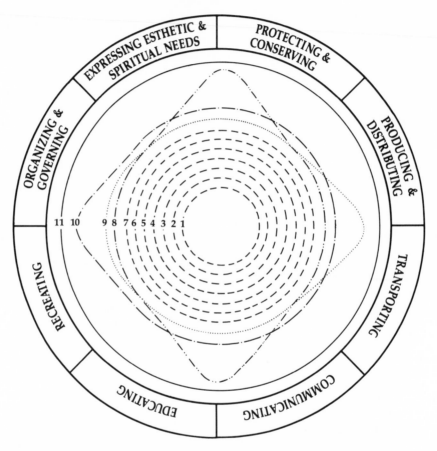

1. Family Community
2. School Community
3. Neighborhood Community
4. Local Community
5. State Community
6. Region-of-States Community
7. National Community

8. United States and
   Inter-American Community
9. United States and
   Atlantic Community
10. United States and
    Pacific Community
11. The World as the
    Home of Mankind

This is the way a child's communities grow, and this same outward thrust from the home and family to larger arenas and larger numbers of people is paralleled in the history of the growth of mankind's communities. The earliest community of man was the family; later, family groups joined other families, thus expanding into a clan that occupied a neighborhood, clans joined other adjacent clans to form a local tribe; and tribes later banded together into economic, social, and political states. More recently science and technology gave man greater mastery over communication and transportation, thus facilitated mankind's current movement through walls of state and national isolation outward into newer, ever widening communities.

A community can be thought of as having both structural and functional elements. A community is a consciously assembled group of people living in a defined geographic space within which the processes of human interaction result in the development of basic human activities, appropriate in kind and intensity to meet problems and purposes of the members of the community. For example, grouped together thus into communities, men have found it easier to protect themselves against harm, to provide food, shelter, and clothing, or to satisfy their needs for spiritual expression.

The family, for instance, exhibits both the functional and structural characteristics of a community. It exists functionally as a biological group required for procreation and for rearing of the young, and it also exists voluntarily for the mutual advantage of its members. A variety of structural arrangements is illustrated in matriarchy and patriarchy.

A community then, not only has size of area and number of people but can be described as a condition in which these people living in the same arena find they have purposes in common. As a community they face common problems, have common interests, and must share common understandings, attitudes, and behaviors if they are to work together to meet their needs.

It is clear that one holding such a conception of a series of expanding communities finds unacceptable the current and erroneous idea brought out in much educational discussion, that community refers only to the local arena. School people must accept the idea of multiple communities and deliberately prepare children and youth for membership in each and every one of the arenas.

Coordination: The Fourth Step

The fourth step in curriculum designing combines the content of the scope with the emphases of the sequence. To illustrate this process of curricular coordination we will combine the diagrams we used in discussing the basic human activities (Chart 1) and the expanding communities of men (Chart 2).

If we lay down our basic human activities wheel and scribe thereon the eleven concentric circles representing the expanding communities of man, then the interrelatedness of the scope and sequence of this particular curricular design becomes apparent. (See Chart 3.)

You will notice that the band between any two circles—representing a particular community—cuts across all eight basic human activities. This suggests that the teacher in treating the community emphasis for which he is responsible, consciously selects experiences calculated to develop pupil understanding and behavior related to each of the several clusters of human activity.

To illustrate this idea more specifically, let us look at Chart 4 which represents one enlarged segment of Chart 3.

You will notice that the radii lines of the scope wheel and the parallel arcs of the concentric circles bound a definite space. This segment of the band suggests to a teacher that one focus of study for his class could be concerned with transporting people and goods within the pupil's local community. In turn, this focus is (1) related to other segments of scope within this local community emphasis, (2) is founded on a prior focus dealing with the segment of transporting in the neighborhood community, studied in a previous grade, and (3) foreshadows subsequent foci dealing with the segment of transporting to be developed in subsequent emphases in later grades. Within this particular focus of study the teacher and pupils would plan the anticipated pupil outcomes in accord with their objectives and would decide upon the content and activities from which they would build their experiences.

There are a number of principles that must be held clearly in mind when creating a curricular design that is based on this particular scope and sequence. The first principle is that the sequence of emphases can be assigned to grades within different school systems by any criteria a system sets up with but one exception: **the particular sequence of expanding communities should be followed in logical order.** Flexibility as to the particular grade in which a community emphasis is treated is permissible. The flexibility depends upon levels of maturation and back-

CHART 3
A SOCIAL STUDIES CURRICULUM DESIGN

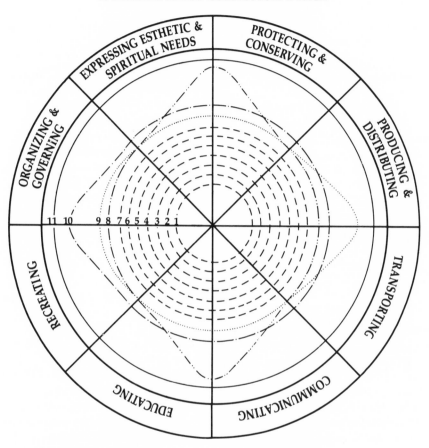

1. Family Community
2. School Community
3. Neighborhood Community
4. Local Community
5. State Community
6. Region-of-States Community
7. National Community

8. United States and Inter-American Community
9. United States and Atlantic Community
10. United States and Pacific Community
11. The World as the Home of Mankind

CHART 4
TRANSPORTATION: THE RELATION BETWEEN COMMUNITIES

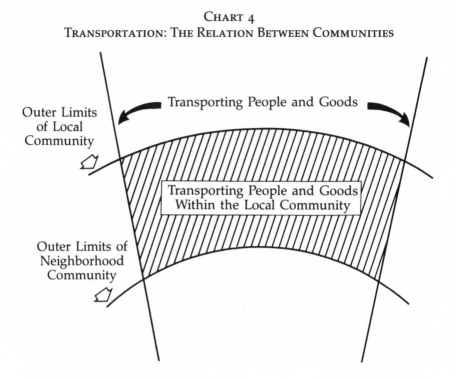

grounds of experience of particular classes of pupils. There is nothing sacred in the idea that the national community should be studied in the fifth grade or that the Inter-American community should be studied in the sixth. Some schools might, for their own particular reasons, wish to study them both in the fifth grade; other schools might cover the national community in the fourth and the next in the fifth. This variation is entirely proper psychologically as no one rigid allocation of community emphasis to grades will fit all children in all schools. The important principle lies in leading the child through these community experiences in a sequence that is both logically and psychologically systematic.

A second principle has already been introduced: **each expanding community deals with the same list of basic human activities but treats each according to the interests and problems pertinent to that particular community.** Within the family community, for instance, all the basic human activities are carried on within the limits of time and effort that the child's family can put into them. Those aspects of the basic human activities which lie beyond the power or capacity of the family (as a lesser community) to engage in successfully on its own are therefore provided for by cooperative activity in a greater community. To illustrate: consider how the family protects itself by locking the doors and windows of the house. Yet, it takes neighborhood cooperation to secure proper street lighting which will boost the degree of protection at night. And only the next larger, the local community, can afford the effort and money to provide squad-car patrols and radio communications for protecting the family, the neighborhood, and the local community. As we are well aware, a local community can provide itself with excellent protection facilities that might be partly nullified unless the next larger community deals with the problem of the criminal who moves freely from area to area. For this reason, the state community has its police force to handle problems beyond the powers of lesser communities. Then states, too, find they cannot provide all the elements of protection required; criminals move from state to state, and to prevent this circumstance from being an unwarranted protection to criminals, regions of states enter into agreements for sharing information, seeking out criminals, and returning them to states that wish to prosecute them. Finally, we find our national community engaged in protecting us in many ways that could not be effectively handled by any lesser community or any combination of lesser communities. The members of a family, the citizens of a local community, the residents of a state, all find that the Federal Bureau of Investigation serves them directly through national action and indirectly through cooperative action with lesser communities.

From this example we see how the increasing interests and needs which the members of a larger community share in common, force that community through either private agency or public institution to develop protective arrangements that are more complex and extended than in lesser communities. The same feature can be found if we trace any one of the basic human activities in its particular form and function through the expanding communities of man.

The implication for educational experiences seems quite clear: each basic human activity is treated in a manner pertinent to the needs of each expanded community. This is to say that within the design we are now discussing, **transporting** cannot be studied once and for all in any particular grade. Within this scope and sequence, each basic human activity is examined in each expanded arena as a new aspect of a familiar problem.

A third principle: **membership in any one of these communities should not be in conflict with membership in others.** Each community has its own structure and functions, paralleled but not duplicated by the other communities. The purpose, range, and complexity of functions are different for each of the communities, yet each reinforces the other. Each American citizen, from the very fact that he is a citizen of the United States, is simultaneously a member of a family, of a neighborhood, of a local area, of a state, of a region of states, and of our national community. Beyond this, each citizen is a member of several larger-than-national communities in the sense that his lesser communities cannot provide solutions to all his problems. As our interests and activities leap over the boundaries of our national community, so they bring us into some more-than-national association with other peoples. With these people we share social, political, and economic problems of such magnitude and complexity that the facilities of a single national community are insufficient to solve them. This is not to say that we are citizens of these enlarged, region-of-nations communities in the sense that we are citizens of the U.S.A., but we share common interests with at least four communities larger in area and population than our national community. (See Chart 2.) A study of our interests in each of these larger communities, however, must not introduce conflict with loyalty to our national community.

A fourth principle deals largely with the nature of child learning but is definitely related to curriculum design. If it is a task of the school to provide pupils with ample first-hand experiences from which come the foundations for other, more vicarious learnings, then the **home, school, neighborhood, and local communities provide the best environment in which initial meanings can be developed.** As the child leaves the more immediate community emphases of the primary grades, he is introduced rapidly to curriculum materials that may not have available abundant first-hand experiences. The learning in the middle grades often loses some vividness and reality as vicarious experiences take up more and more of the pupil's school time. The transition from the pupils' immediate communities with their wealth of first-hand experience to the more remote communities of state, region, and nation requires very special attention to the connections between what the child learned from the family, school, neighborhood, and local communities and what he might learn about things with which he cannot always have direct personal contact. The curriculum design we are illustrating builds upon these first-hand experiences provided in the immediate communities, those latter meanings, understandings, and comparisons which are necessary for generalizing about other, greater communities of man.

At the same time, it should be recognized that the experiences dealing with these greater, more remote communities need not be exclusively vicarious. To use the national community as an example, many of the activities carried on in this emphasis affect the lives of pupils found in any classroom. A nation-wide strike of workers in transportation or a serious drought in the corn belt can deeply affect the social and economic life of children and their families. In making use of what is real in the lives of these pupils and their families, the teacher can guide pupil interest in such firsthand experiences into understanding of the interdependence of people within the national community. Such personally connected experiences constitute the impetus for dealing with many more vicarious experiences necessary to fuller understanding of the national arena.

A fifth principle: **any single community emphasized for study in a particular grade has both central and peripheral areas of attention.** Within the community assigned to a grade for special study, there will occur some phases of human activities that more properly belong to the peripheral communities assigned to later grades for emphasis. Pupil interest in these peripheral activities sometimes poses a problem for the teacher. The fascinating transcontinental airliners fly over the first graders studying the family community; the state senator visits the third grade absorbed in the affairs of the local community; a TV depicts the President of the United States in conference with the heads of other nations for fourth graders focusing on the basic human activities within their state community.

Such stimulating events and the interest aroused in alert pupils cannot be denied nor ignored. But neither should these peripheral experiences attain the center of attention and thus replace the emphasis on the lesser community assigned to the grade by the entire staff in the planned-in-advance aspect of social studies design. The focus of study in the **local community** emphasis, for example, with regard to transporting people and goods, is **not** aviation in all its global aspects, is **not** the national system of railroads, but **is** focused upon the transporting of peoples and goods through use of a local system of streets and roads, through local taxi and bus services, through local commuter train schedules, through local harbors and airport facilities, and the like. The peripheral events and resulting pupil interests suggested earlier can be used by the skillful teacher as the leads for building readiness for the next larger communities of men which pupils anticipate as emphases for study in later grades.

The phases of transporting that are clearly state, regional, or national are admitted in that grade studying the local community, and their relationship to local activities is established. But in the local community emphasis, the focus of attention is placed upon the efforts of people in the pupils' town, city, or county, and the metropolitan area to meet the needs of the local community for transportation services. In the study in each community emphasis, phases related to other community emphases will exist and these should receive some attention; it should be clearly held in mind, however, that these peripheral interests are not the center of attention in studying the basic human activities of that particular community emphasized at a given grade.

A sixth principle: **each community has historical dimensions that give perspective to contemporary social, economic, and political conditions within that community.** Each community—family, local, state, national, or whatever—has in its genesis and its history the factors that condition the current ongoing life of that community. For instance, each family has its history. The pupil who views pictures of his parents when they were children in the arms of their parents—the pupil's grandparents—begins to understand that all adults were once children. The first grader learns that as children, his parents grew up in times and under conditions that were very different from those of today.

This increasing understanding of historical change must be nurtured in the pupil by the teacher who guides him to reach into the past and, in a degree appropriate to his maturity, to trace the roots of his community and to study its development. It is thus that the pupil gains perspective with regard to each of the basic human activities. To use an obvious example, transporting was once entirely a matter of human muscle power. As man created containers, floated logs on the streams, and trained his animals to carry his loads—so transporting became only partially a matter of human muscle power. Man more recently constructed steamships, railroad cars, automobiles, and airplanes. He has harnessed steam, expanding gases, electricity, and nuclear power to drive these new vehicles.

The teacher and his pupils can hardly avoid considering the history underlying the development of each community of men and each cluster of basic human activities if the understanding and the behavior desired for citizenship are adequately to be realized.

With these six principles for coordinating scope and sequence held clearly in mind, we can now move on to an emphasis-by-emphasis consideration of the possibilities for teaching-learning experiences within this social studies design.

The Family Community:
Emphasis No. 1

You will notice (in Chart 3) that the central circle, representing the family community, includes a segment or wedge of each basic human activity. Within this family community we find parents protecting the health and lives of their children. The activity of educating is evident as older siblings and adults instruct infants in learning to eat, walk, or talk; recreation is provided for all family members; and religious and aesthetic expressions find many outlets. The family organizes in different ways to suit different purposes; members communicate with each other almost constantly; and the family transports itself on many occasions. The family produces, distributes, and consumes many goods and services. The family obviously engages to some degree in each of the eight basic human activities.

The family, however, cannot through its own efforts provide for all its needs, so some must be met through the basic human activities as carried out by other larger communities. The most pertinent illustration for an audience of teachers would be the difference in providing education as carried on in the family community and in the school community.

The School Community:
Emphasis No. 2

If we draw the next circle and look closely at the band representing the school community, we see that the school also engages in each and every cluster of human activites. Schools are obviously organized for and are engaged in providing education. Play time provides recreation; the school nurse and the fire drill provide protection, and communicating within the building is essential to the life of the school. Transportation is provided to and from school, whether by "shank's mare," bicycle, family car, or school bus. Pupils are encouraged to express aesthetic impulses, and spiritual values are stressed in holiday celebrations, flag salutes, etc. Producing, distributing, and consuming activities can be noted in such activities as hot lunch programs, and in the fruit juice or milk break.

The Neighborhood Community:
Emphasis No. 3

When we draw in the circle which defines the band representing the neighborhood community, we see how each of the communities expands from the previous and enlarges the pupil's relationships with all the basic human activities. At this stage, it is also easy to understand that the individual is a member of each of these communities and that there is no fundamental conflict involved in this multiple community membership.

Within this community of the child's neighborhood are rich first-hand experiences useful to an understanding of man's activities in meeting his needs. The branch bank in the neighborhood keeps his money, the neighborhood fire station protects his life and property, and the corner gas station services his family means of transportation. The child's school provides education and recreational facilities for all neighborhood community members; communicating is carried on over back fences, through the corner mailbox, and by sending small boys on errands; the neighborhood shopping center distributes the goods and services consumed by families and the school. Without question, the neighborhood is a community that influences the education of children to a great extent.

The Local Community: Emphasis No. 4

As we draw in the next circle which forms a band representing the local community, it would be well to point out that, according to local conditions, this community could be termed a town, a city, a county, or a metropolitan area. The local community is composed of all the neighborhoods that touch each other in this larger population complex.

The local community fairly teems with possibilities for direct experiences suitable for this social studies program. There are multiple examples, both private and public, of human activities appropriate for study in this arena. There is a host of examples of producing, distributing, and consuming to be found in the interurban rail and bus systems: communicating can be studied through the local telephone exchange, or the exciting media of the local press, radio, and TV stations. The town, city, county, or metropolitan area system of government can be experienced directly by pupils; recreational opportunities abound in the civic center or the zoo; and understanding of education can be gained through finding out how the county or city school system serves all of the children within the local arena.

Many teachers find the local community an appropriate emphasis in which to begin systematic attention to historical perspective. Every community has had its beginnings and its story of growth. In considering the history of the local community, many teachers mistakenly assume that the historical grass is greener in some storybook community, but this social studies design suggests that there are more exciting first-hand historical experiences to be had in the pupil's own local community.

The State Community:
Emphasis No. 5

As we sketch in the next band, the state community, one is conscious of the particular manner in which the public and private sectors of the state pick up each of the basic human activities and expand them in ways that are impossible for the smaller populations of the lesser communities within the state. In the state arena one thinks of protecting in terms of the state police force, of conserving in terms of state associations of tree farmers or of insurance underwriters, or of transporting in terms of the state system of highways and of feeder airlines that connect the larger population centers of the state. One sees in the mind's eye the state department of education and the state library system as agencies providing educational services; the state Chamber of Commerce, state Council of Labor Unions, or the state Association of Wholesalers, as illustrative of producing and distributing goods and services; or the state parks and beaches as examples of providing recreation facilities beyond the ability of lesser communities. The various religious denominations have state-wide conferences and programs; and the state capitol is a rich resource in its legislative, executive, and judicial branches which demonstrate organizing and governing activities.

The state community has a time dimension of a great interest and import to children. Not only is the school responsible for developing understanding of the state of today and tomorrow, but also for helping pupils comprehend antecedent conditions and events that shaped the state of today. Who lived in this arena before our ancestors came to settle here? How did these earlier people, generally Indians, carry on the basic human activities? How did the early settlers transport themselves and their livestock and household possessions to the new land? What resources did they extract from the soil, the sea, the mine, and forest to feed, clothe, and house themselves? What new tools and technics were invented or borrowed that changed the earlier ways of communicating, transporting, protecting, producing, etc., within the arena we call our state? The possibilities of historic study in discovering the cause of current state activities are rich and almost endless. The teacher and his pupils have great latitude, during the planning-in-process, in deciding what clusters of human activities to pursue and in what order within this emphasis on their state community.

The Region-of-States Community:
Emphasis No. 6

The next band represents the region-of-states community. The people of the United States were once much concerned about sectionalism and fought a regrettable war in which nationalism triumphed and sectionalism dwindled.

Recently we have seen a realistic approach to certain problems that cut across state lines but are not universal enough to be appropriately considered as national problems. This approach can be termed regionalism and has been found an effective instrument filling a gap between the inability of states to deal with certain problems and the nation which is busy with more universal concerns. There has been much in the press about the Colorado River. Yet in spite of the arguments among the states over the use of the waters of this river, we find it successfully tapped for industrial and domestic use in the entire state of Colorado, in southern Nevada, in the Yuma area of Arizona, in the Imperial and Coachella Valleys of California, and in the city of Los Angeles. Without the cooperative efforts of the several states that consider themselves as a region of states sharing this river wealth, the dams, aqueducts, and canals necessary for distributing this water would never have been built.

The United States National Community:
Emphasis No. 7

As we scribe the great band representing the national community, we are aware once more that the child must come to see the interrelationships existing between communities contained within it. This is true of the historical as well as the contemporary insights. These insights are further developed as special attention is given to the history of our nation. We must understand that problems and interests examined in this seventh emphasis leap over the limits of state and regional communities and bring people together into national association. There is a "weness" about 170,000,000 Americans that must be appreciated and understood by all competent citizens.

In the study of this national community we guide pupils through appropriate experiences, to grasp the magnitude of our continental railway systems that carry us from Los Angeles to New York without changing trains. In this emphasis we study a national postal system, a national organization of law enforcement, national systems of producing, distributing, and consuming goods and services that provide what we are pleased to term "the good life." All of the basic human activities are studied as satisfying our national needs.

Here, too, we note that the pupil who has drawn the corresponding elements from experiences with many lesser communities is the one who can synthesize experiences into a sound understanding of a national community which is so far flung that he cannot deal with much of it in a first-hand manner. It is this pupil who has a background of social, economic, and political understanding of and behavior in lesser communities who can adequately generalize about this greater community and recognize the uniqueness of its ways of carrying out the basic human activities within the national arena.

The United States and Inter-American Community: Emphasis No. 8

If we draw our next community band in the form of a north-south ellipse, we encompass both North and South America in what we term the United States and Inter-American community. That such a community exists should not be a controversial question for anyone who is informed. We have long sought the friendliest of ties with other Americans. This cooperation is reflected in our police-free borders, north and south; in the St. Lawrence River Waterway, and in the northern radar warning system that serves both the United States and Canada, in the Pan American Union and in the Organization of American States; in our willingness to invest some 18 billion dollars in the economies of these other American countries. Without common concern, common need, and common effort, we could not have an Alcan highway, a Pan-American highway, Pan-American Olympic Games, or even enjoy our coffee and our Latin American music!

The United States and Atlantic Community: Emphasis No. 9

As we draw our next elliptical band from the west coast of the United States eastward across the Atlantic we define the next emphasis—that of the United States and Atlantic community. This community is made up of the United States, Europe, the Middle East, and Africa. Here again we find close ties already existing with other free nations and we cooperate with them in carrying out essential activities. Also, we find problems of co-existing with nations that do not value, as we do, the individual and free institutions. We draw sharp contrasts between different forms of government and different ideas about the nature and rights of man.

We see the results of men's efforts in this community to provide the conditions and facilities that meet the common needs of nations. The North Atlantic Treaty Organization, the European Coal and Steel Community, and the other working agreements are known to you by virtue of their prominent position in the news of our day. In all of the basic human activities new arrangements and institutions, both public and private, are emerging to bind the peoples of the U.S. and Atlantic community together.

The United States and Pacific Community:
Emphasis No. 10

Our final ellipse starts at our eastern seaboard and extends westward to include most of Asia and all of Australia. This band we call the United States and Pacific community. It can be likened in many respects to the preceding community for in it we find both free and slave nations. With these free nations we seek to build a cooperative community in which the efforts of our and their public and private agencies will serve to satisfy our mutual needs. With the slave nations, however, we seek to maintain a condition of co-existence.

The Southeast Asian Treaty Organization, the Columbo nations, and the efforts of the International Cooperation Administration stand as tributes to the mutual confidence and good-will existing between the United States and certain other national communities in this arena. The basic human activities that make us members of this emerging community are reflected in the rapidly increasing economic connections we share with the Pacific peoples in producing and distributing goods and services and in maintaining with them the air and sea means of transporting goods and people.

In considering these larger-than-national communities we should ask whether our membership in any one of these communities is in conflict with membership in any other. It is relatively easy to see how the human activities of the national, regional, state, local, and lesser communities parallel but do not duplicate the activities of other communities. We are not only members of each lesser-than-national community, but we are citizens of each. Beyond the national borders, however, each American citizen is involved in larger communities even if he isn't aware of it. We need raw materials from other parts of the world to maintain our economy. They in turn need our commodities, friendship, and even protection. With these peoples we share economic, social, and political problems of such complexity that the facilities of a single nation are insufficient to solve them.

The United States and the World as the Home of Mankind: Emphasis No. 11

Lastly, the great band that encircles all the lesser communities is coterminous with our earth. Within this arena the human family of 2.7 billion people spreads unevenly over the surface of the land. Mounting population is pushing the limits of earth's resources to sustain so many. As the natural barriers of mountain, desert, or sea are bridged, lesser communities of men with differing ideals and institutions come into direct contact with one another. The tensions resulting have caused two recent world wars and threaten us with yet more tragic ones to come. For such a confused setting, men try to invent laws and institutions and technics that will reduce conflict and prevent war.

There are many approaches to the social, economic, and political problems that affect all of mankind. The United Nations and its agencies of Food and Agriculture Organization, World Health Organization, Security Council, and Social and Economic Council are efforts to work out our common destiny with peace and justice.

In the private sector, industrialists, artists, scientists, sportsmen, spiritual leaders, and a host of groups with common interests and values have formed associations to promote their joint welfare. In each of the basic human activities we see the beginnings of customs and institutions out of which could possibly emerge a world association of free peoples that would hold in check any anarchistic group or nation from destroying the peace and order of the earth.

Pupils need to have carefully selected and directed learning experiences that will prepare them to participate in creating the policy and in administrating the public and private efforts in this emerging human community.

In Summary

In retrospect, we can see how the expanding, concentric communities cut across all the basic human activities of men living in these arenas. Within this curriculum design for social studies it is possible to fuse the needs of society and of the child into educative experiences designed not for mere accumulation of information, but rather designed for developing the understanding and attitude that form the core of competent citizenship behavior. Within such a curricular framework, our schools have the opportunity to foster the creative potential of each individual child and at the same time build the basic understanding and behavior required in common by all citizens. Experiences with the full range of basic human activities would be the consciously held responsibility of each teacher—from kindergarten through the secondary school. The full range of expanding communities of men from the family to the nation to the world would be treated systematically and assure each citizen the preparation for fuller participation in the several community arenas in which he lives simultaneously.

We can be certain of peace and security in the coming years only as men universally hold in common great ideals, sound plans, and essential skills of cooperative action. The survival and progress of our democratic and representative way of life demand that the elementary [and secondary] schools give pupils experiences in each and every human activity in each and every expanding community of men.

We can sum up much of what we said in the words of John Childs. This philosopher contends that we need a balance in our curriculum. He says:

> I consider it important for American educators to recognize that devotion to the ideals of democracy in no way bars us from making a deliberate effort to nurture the young in the essential patterns of democratic life and thought. If our schools are to serve as positive agencies for the maintenance of a 'free' society, they must be concerned today with 'society' as well as with the 'child,' with 'subject-matter' as well as with 'method,' with 'product' as well as with 'process,' with human 'responsibilities' as well as with human 'freedoms,' and with social and moral 'ends' as well as with classroom 'procedures' and educational 'means.'[6]

You in this audience, and the unseen numbers of educators you represent, have it in your power to draw from society and from childhood the materials for a curriculum design that will respect the individuality of learning while assuring the survival and progress of the values and institutions we hold so dear.

Notes

1. Exodus 12:26.

2. California State Central Committee on the Social Studies, *Minutes of Meetings* (Sacramento, Calif.: State Department of Education, 1956).

3. Malcolm P. Douglass, "Interrelationships between Man and the Natural Environment for Use in the Geographic Strand of the Social Studies Curriculum" (Stanford, Calif.: Unpublished Doctoral Thesis, 1954).

4. *The United States in the World Today*, edited by Clyde F. Kohn, appeared in 1957.

5. John Dewey, *Experience and Education* (New York: Macmillan, 1948), p. 65.

6. John L. Childs, *Education and Morals* (New York: Appleton-Century-Crofts, 1950), p. ix.

The second paper in this set, reprinted from The Nation's Schools *(September 1958), proposes a "standard national curriculum" based on the scheme of expanding concentric circles of communities (sketched in the first paper).*

The article brought a flood of comments to the editor, Arthur H. Rice. A sampling of these comments was published in the November 1958 issue of The Nation's Schools. *Many writers pointed out the dangers of a standard national curriculum. Realizing the logic of these cautions, I began to rethink the problem.*

I have since come to agree that decisions in curriculum and instruction must finally be the choices of local and state communities (for reasons amplified in Chapter 4). I do not agree, however, with those who argue that there are no basic values or concepts in American culture that can be taught. Yes, we believe in diversity, but diversity is one of the fundamental tenets of our democracy along with freedom, liberty, justice, equality of opportunity, and the rule of law. Unless we agree on such fundamental premises, and teach our young to understand and defend these values, there is a distinct probability that our culture will not survive the contest with the beliefs of authoritarian or autocratic parties. Since the time of the founding fathers our literature has clearly stated that certain common values and a shared knowledge are essential to our society. We must succeed in identifying our curricular goals and in providing guidelines for educators that will allow them to perform their duties through a variety of instructional approaches.

Families need guidelines as well as teachers. The recent changes in family life have sometimes led to a disturbing lack of input into the values and lifestyles of our young people. The education of our youth is as much the responsibility of the family as of the schools. A set of shared values and basic knowledge prepared for our schools could also be of great importance for family members. Part of America's strength has traditionally flowed from the cooperation of family and educators in teaching common values, concepts, and behavior to our young.

Design for a
National Curriculum*

2

These questions must be answered:

In a world as troubled as ours, do we not have to agree on a curriculum design that will at least expose all children in our nation to a common set of values and to a common fund of knowledge?

Can our precious liberties and the right of the individual to be different be protected by a people whose education may not have prepared them to hold in common a belief in such ideals?

Can a curriculum conceived primarily by the state board and the local school district and administered typically by the individual teacher provide adequate foundations for the nation's strength and welfare?

Can we hope to survive as a free people unless our enculturation includes the most significant generalizations from the frontiers of knowledge?

These are questions pointedly asked by laymen and educators alike, questions for which suitable answers must be found.

During the last 25 years we have witnessed a splintering of the curriculum in American public schools as each school district has insisted on curricular independence. A further discontinuity in curriculum has

---

*Reprinted from *The Nation's Schools* 62, nos. 3 and 5 (September and November 1958).

been encouraged as certain educational leaders have stressed the "right" of each teacher to select such teaching-learning experiences as he personally sees fit with little regard for the team role assigned him in the school's curricular pattern.

Finally, the school curriculum has not thrust its roots deeply into the fertile subsoil of the humanities, social sciences, sciences, and mathematics. Too often, curriculum planners have been satisfied with the superficial content that feeds the whims and interests of the moment.

The net result of this curricular dilemma is all too obvious: The American schools are not in agreement on which understandings, attitudes and competencies should be the minimum but universal enculturation of our children and youth. There is no truly American curricular design of significant content and suitable learning experiences on which the nation can rely for creating the universal understanding of loyalty to the values, laws and institutions essential to perpetuate and improve the way of life of a free people.

We are not for a moment advocating that the lesser than national communities should not be treated fully in the school curriculum. Obviously each of the concentric circle communities of men (family community, neighborhood community, local community of city or county or metropolitan complex, state community, region-of-states community, national community, the greater regions-of-nations communities, and the inclusive community of humankind) needs to be treated in the school curriculum.

However, we are saying that the state community and the lesser communities within the state are currently well represented by state school boards and county and district school boards whose primary interest has been to provide the curricular design and teaching aids that will better assure common understanding and behavior of our young citizens in these smaller than national communities. So far, in the national community, no comparable public body exists to propose the design for a curriculum that will serve the ends of our national community.[1]

Some Unacceptable Solutions

One proposed solution coming from studies in comparative education would have the national government replace the local school boards and the state educational commissions in determining curriculum design. In such a national system educational objectives would be achieved through a nationwide administration of a single curriculum design controlled by federal fiat. Such a proposal rightly arouses strong fear in freedom loving Americans—fear that a federally operated school system could be used to destroy our way of life if it fell into totalitarian hands.

Promising Solutions

But there are other ways to achieve a design for that part of our school curriculum which develops the common outlook essential for our national survival and progress. The proposal herein advocated draws on the successful experience of several other nonfederal endeavors in our nation: nonpolitical and voluntary cooperative efforts to meet a national need.

We have, for instance, a surprising unanimity of agreement throughout the nation on what constitutes the basic education for the profession of medicine. This agreement has been achieved by the continuing process of study, experimentation and program modification according to plan.

This movement has been led by the Council on Medical Education of the American Medical Association. The power of intelligent analysis and the soundness of proposals for curriculum have persuaded men and institutions to accept a relatively standard design for medical education that has resulted in superior training for these guardians of our national health.

To be sure, we are concerned in this proposal not with a profession's training but with the education of today's children, tomorrow's citizens, and this latter problem is vastly more complex and more crucial to the nation's welfare. The lesson to be drawn from the experience of medical education is simply this: It is possible to gain national agreement through the efforts of nonpolitical and voluntary agencies.

Establish a Laboratory

Let us return to the problem of a curriculum design to meet our national needs. It is my proposal that an existing center or laboratory be selected or a new one be created at which, during a two year period, the problem be examined and that there be produced a series of fundamental papers on the national curriculum design. These papers would then be used widely to stimulate a curriculum discussion by laymen and educators throughout the national community. Undoubtedly there are many conceivable plans, any one of which might serve the functions herein considered. However, we have confidence that such a plan of operation as is outlined here could succeed.

Select a Team

The proposed Center could select for 1959–60 and possibly for 1960–61 30 fellows who would be competent, and deeply interested in focusing on the curriculum problem. Among the fellows thus committed, 15 might be specialists in cultural anthropology, sociology, political science, economics, human geography, demography, social psychology, jurisprudence, philosophy, history, public health, biological sciences, physical sciences, mathematics, language, literature, music, the arts, and so forth.

Each fellow, possessing broad competence in one of the foregoing foundations of school curriculum, would be selected because of his willingness to work as a team member on the identifying and the organizing of generalizations from his area that would probably become an integral part of the school curriculum.

The Center would at the same time select 10 fellows who are expert in school curriculum theory and practice. These school curriculum experts could be chosen from the universities, from state, county and city school systems, and from private schools. They would be competent in biopsychological theory of learning, in growth and development, in curriculum design, and in school administration.

The Center would select another five fellows who have had outstandingly successful experience in representing the laymen through local and state school boards, P.T.A.'s and similar government and voluntary groups.

These 10 fellows in school curriculum and five lay fellows would work closely with the 15 fellows in the foundations, but it would be the special contribution of the 10 curriculum fellows and five lay fellows to examine thoroughly the patterns by which the generalizations considered most significant by their 15 colleagues could be structured for school use. The team of 30, concentrating on the school curriculum problem, would together outline the task and procedures for the subgroups working on the two phases suggested. The 30 fellows conceivably could make a solid beginning on this massive problem during the first year, 1959–60. Their work might culminate in a number of papers published by individual fellows, teams of fellows, or by the group as a whole.

One of the more specific outcomes of the 1959–60 effort should be mature proposals for the consideration of a second group similar in character to the 1959–60 group which would be assembled for the year 1960–61. Some overlap for 1959–60 and 1960–61 personnel would be desirable.

The second year of this enterprise should carry forward and enrich and refine the work of the first group. Out of this second year could come a document presenting a comprehensive curriculum design for the entire nation.

Such a fundamental statement on the school curriculum could then become the object of wide and intensive study by lay and professional groups throughout the nation.

Create a Permanent Center

Eventually, we see the desirability of creating a permanent national center, or perhaps several such national centers in universities and/or in national organizations of educators and of lay citizens, continuously to examine the exploding frontiers of human thought and endeavor for the purpose of identifying those generalizations that should be incorporated into the school curriculum design as guides to teacher selections of pupil experiences.

The preliminary and foundational works of the 60 fellows at the Center during 1959–61 would be of inestimable value to any subsequent effort of the proposed permanent national curriculum center or centers.

It might be wise to test the soundness of this whole proposal by holding a five-day conference at the Center initially selected for the two-year study in late autumn of 1958. To such a conference might be invited a carefully selected panel of experts in the humanities, social sciences, sciences and mathematics, each one of whom indicates an interest in school curriculum. Likewise to such a conference should be invited leading curriculum theorists and practitioners and lay leaders from school boards and other citizens groups.

During such a late autumn conference three objectives would be uppermost in the mind of the Center administrative personnel:

1. Is the proposal for a two-year effort on a national curriculum design of high significance?
2. Can a workable two-year plan of action be prepared?
3. Who are the most likely candidates for fellowships?

There is widespread concern that the schools of this nation may not be providing sufficient common understanding of, loyalty to, and competence in our democratic way of life to assure its survival against the threat of internal and external forces of disintegration. We propose that a Center be selected or created to devote its potential (or a part of it) for a two-year period to a study of the national curriculum problem, hoping that the effort will result in a challenging, sound, and prestige-laden statement. This statement would deal in fundamental ways with the national problem of selection and arrangement of content and teaching-learning experiences.

From this beginning it is hoped that a curriculum design would emerge that would give greatest assurance of the survival and progress of the values, laws, and institutions of free peoples.

Timetable for Designing a National Curriculum

Autumn 1958
Five-day conference to find out:

1. Whether the proposal for a two-year effort on a national curriculum design is of high significance.

2. Whether a workable two-year plan of action can be prepared and endorsed.

3. Who are the most likely candidates for 1959–60.

Year 1959–60
Purpose: To draw up preliminary proposals for a national curriculum design.

1. A team composed of 15 specialists in as many major subject matter fields;

2. Ten fellows who are specialists in curriculum theory and practice, and five lay fellows.

Goal: A series of papers to be published by individual fellows, teams of fellows, or the group of 30 as a whole. These statements would serve as a basis for wide discussion of the problem by laymen and educators.

Year 1960–61

Purpose: To formulate a more mature proposal for a national curriculum design, using the papers of the first group of fellows and the subsequent criticisms as the starting point.

Personnel: A second team composed of 15 fellows who are competent in the substantive fields, 10 fellows who are leaders in curriculum designing, and five lay fellows, with some carryover from the first team.

Goal: A second and comprehensive curriculum design for intensive study by interested groups and individuals throughout the nation.

Future

Purpose: To establish a permanent, nonfederal National Curriculum Center or several such Centers whose goal would be the continuous examination of the exploding frontiers of human thought and achievement and to identify generalizations that must be incorporated into the national curriculum design.

WHAT LEADERS THINK ABOUT A "DESIGN FOR A NATIONAL CURRICULUM"

Competent Approach . . .

Norman M. Cousins, Editor, *Saturday Review*

Many thanks for the privilege of reading Dr. Hanna's proposals for meeting the national curriculum problem. It seems to me Dr. Hanna presents a straightforward, uncomplicated, competent approach to the problem. He does not attempt to dictate a standard for curriculum reform; what he does try to do is to define the machinery which is essential in any concerted and imaginative attack on the problem on a national scale. I am glad to support his efforts.

Local Initiative First . . .

Lawrence G. Derthwick, Commissioner of Education, U.S. Department of Health, Education and Welfare

At the time when there is a growing interest on the part of the American public in the critical role of education as a key to both national welfare and national security, it is highly important that much experimental thinking and planning be done in the field of education. However, it is my own belief that the national interest in education can best be met through our great American tradition of creative diversity. Thus, local initiative and planning closely coordinated with national organizations and groups can lead to the same basic goals proposed by Dr. Hanna.

Dangerous Assumption . . .

W. W. Charters, Jr., Associate Professor, Graduate Institute of Education, and Social Psychologist, Washington University, St. Louis

The substance of Dr. Hanna's proposal is innocuous. Few will object to a thoughtful study of curriculum problems however it may occur, so long as there is no obligation to buy the product. Beware, however, in accepting the proposal lest we accept the argument in which it is couched. Dr. Hanna confronts us with a dangerous tacit assumption: that we must place our trust for curriculum planning in the expert. Apparently, he sees curriculum planning as a technical problem in medical education where reasonable unanimity exists regarding the ends of training but this does not parallel the case of public education. Here the tough problem is in formulating ends, and not in the highly general phrasing of Dr. Hanna's "loyalty," "understanding," or "common outlook essential for national survival," which have all meanings for all men. Yet it is this nontechnical task which Dr. Hanna would have us turn over to a national panel consisting predominantly of the subject-matter experts and curriculum specialists.

In my mind the abrogation of citizen responsibility to the expert in so many realms of public life represents a social trend more insidious than centralized political control, against which Dr. Hanna guards. Centralized control at least has its checks and balances in the political process. By blaming failure in developing a national curriculum on local experts ("educational leaders," "teachers," and "curriculum planners") and by assigning responsibility to a panel of supertechnicians, Dr. Hanna tacitly implies reliance upon the expert.

Rather than encourage the trend, American education should choose to counteract it in deed as well as in word. Decision regarding the ends of public education is the responsibility of citizens to whom the schools belong, and the best interests of society will be served if it so remains.

Let's Define Design . . .

David D. Henry, President, University of Illinois

The key word in Dr. Hanna's "Design for a National Curriculum" is "design."

If "designing" a curriculum is conceived to be the identification of unifying principles and basic objectives, constructive and useful reports would undoubtedly emerge from the proposed center for curriculum study. On the other hand, if the group of fellows and other experts should consider their task to be to outline specific subject matter, I fear the results would not be worth the effort needed for organization.

The search for wide acceptance of common values, ideals and attitudes related to the conservation and development of our democratic way is a fundamental concern of the schools. We shall not find these hoped-for outcomes of the school experience, however, in any definition of specific information to be taught. A basic body of knowledge should be a common expectation, of course, but there is no automatic formation of values, ideals and attitudes from content alone, or any one prescription of content. The methods for achieving the goals outlined and the materials which should be utilized in the teaching process must in large part be left to the individual teacher and to the individual school.

All of this is to endorse Paul Hanna's approach, his analysis of the need for common influences, and the need for a definition of basic goals and objectives, with curricular suggestions related to them. I infer that Dr. Hanna expects no simple result from a curriculum design; rather, that he expects working with curriculum problems in a national center will evolve materials which will stimulate teachers and citizens in local communities in searching for school improvement.

When our schools work for high standards in academic achievement, encourage each student to develop to his full capacity intellectually, and have this stress upon the intellectual rooted in a curriculum based upon the humanities, the social studies, mathematics and the sciences, we are a long way toward the goal which Dr. Hanna has outlined. In such a setting, with appropriate evaluation, a curriculum study of the kind proposed would be very useful. Without such a setting, any "design" will have limited use.

In short, attitudes, values, ideals emerge from the total school experience and the context of the local community. This experience can be influenced by a definition of what is desirable in a common approach; but the final responsibility for citizen development is in the local community.

Restrained Enthusiasm . . .

V. O. Key, Jr., Professor of Government, Harvard University, and President, American Political Science Association

Dr. Hanna's "Design for a National Curriculum," I regret to say, stirs within me only the most restrained enthusiasm. Of political indoctrination, we already have too much. Doubtless we could better arrange things to feed into the curriculum the new "generalizations" from the "exploding frontiers of thought." I have the most serious reservation, however, whether a National Curriculum Center is the way to accomplish that end.

I should think that a sustained effort to improve the subject-matter training of teachers would be a more suitable mode of attack. In short, if I were a foundation official under the necessity of deciding whether to finance the Center, I would regard some of the ends as most dubious and the means as one not well calculated to achieve the ends, whether desirable or undesirable.

Pioneer Thinking . . .

C. C. Trillingham, Superintendent of Schools, Los Angeles County, and President, American Association of School Administrators

I agree with Dr. Hanna that some values and some learnings are of such consequence and significance that all American children and youth should have access to them through the curriculum. However, I believe that there is now more "commonality" of purpose and program in American schools than the article leads us to believe. This is the result of conferences of education leaders through major professional associations which cut across state lines, the widespread use of basic textbooks and educational films and other instructional aids, the similar requirements of the state legislatures regarding school programs, and the like.

Dr. Hanna is right when he said that the American people generally will not approve a curriculum design fashioned by the federal government or any of its agencies. His proposal for a commission of distinguished specialists and laymen to prepare a tentative program for study and discussion throughout the nation is a most intriguing idea.

Who would select these specialists and laymen?

Would their proposals be accepted by other educators and laymen who are equally qualified?

How would the project be financed? By the individuals involved, their institutions, the federal government, or by foundations?

Would foundations or other agencies be willing to finance the undertaking without any strings attached?

Is it not more desirable to seek common agreement on educational purposes and leave the necessary program development to the states and local communities?

Hasn't our experience convinced us that we don't change the curriculum without changing teachers, and we don't change teachers unless we involve them in the process?

Would it not be more practical to first take one area for study rather than to encompass the whole curriculum?

In spite of my questions and comments, I think Dr. Hanna has done some bold pioneer thinking. The influence of such a venture on classroom practice throughout the country would probably be in proportion to the quality and merit of the thinking and planning that went into the project at all levels.

Has Merit . . .

Jane Franseth, Specialist, Rural Education, U.S. Office of Education, and President, Association for Supervision and Curriculum Development

"Can a national curriculum design actually make a significant contribution to the advancement of education for the maintenance and advancement of a democratic way of life?" This was the question I asked myself as I read Dr. Hanna's proposal. My first response was, "No, I hardly think so, especially if the expectations of the plan include significant improvement of what goes on in schools following a presentation of the new curriculum design."

However, the proposal suggests an approach to curriculum improvement which, in my judgment, has merit. Its purpose is important. Improved understanding of what democracy in our country actually means, it seems to me, is urgent. The preservation and advancement of democracy as a way of life is now more dependent than ever on the quality of education we provide for children and adults.

However, it does not seem realistic to me to expect improvement in the school curriculum through providing a document to the schools which presents a comprehensive curriculum for the entire nation. I would have difficulty believing that the necessary changes could be made by school staff members unless they, too, have had the kinds of opportunities necessary to increase their understanding of the "common set of values" and "common fund of knowledge" that Dr. Hanna talks about.

On the other hand, it seems to me that the outcomes of a three-year project such as the one Dr. Hanna describes would have much to offer schools to facilitate progress in curriculum development. A document describing a proposed curriculum design might be useful as an example and as an important source of knowledge.

Deserves Examination . . .

Neal Gross, Associate Professor of Education and Lecturer on Sociology, Harvard University

Although I would question the wisdom of certain aspects of Dr. Hanna's proposal, I believe the problem to which it is directed is an important one, and therefore that his plan and perhaps other proposals for dealing with it deserve careful examination. I would heartily endorse the idea of a five-day conference to explore the strength and possible shortcomings of Dr. Hanna's extremely interesting plan for a national curriculum design.

Timely . . .

A. John Holden, Commissioner of Education, Vermont, and President, Council of Chief State School Officers

Dr. Hanna's concern for the splintering and superficiality of the American school curriculum is timely. His proposal of a procedure for developing a design for a national curriculum is promising. There may be those who would fear it, as perhaps leading to an imposed uniformity. Yet it calls for no change in the official sanctions governing the curriculum. I believe that unless the profession displays more aggressive and coherent leadership in shaping the curriculum we will have its shape increasingly determined by pressure groups and ill-conceived legislation.

Individual initiative and local freedom will always have an important place in determining what happens in our American schools, but these will be most productive when exercised within a broad framework of national agreement on the general outline, and when informed by the kind of responsible and competent study Dr. Hanna advocates.

If the statements emanating from the proposed Center are to have influence, no matter how "prestige laden," I believe it would be essential that the Center be established under conditions that would secure the confidence of major educational organizations at the outset.

Local Decision . . .

Delmas F. Miller, Principal, University High School, West Virginia University, and Chairman, Curriculum Committee, National Association of Secondary-School Principals

It is true that there would be merit in a nationwide curriculum planning procedure such as Dr. Hanna suggests. Its function would be necessarily advisory. It would be dangerous if it became dictatorial.

The schools of America are still "grass root," and what children are taught will necessarily remain a local decision.

Much Impressed . . .

Charles L. Anspach, President, Central Michigan College

I am much impressed with Dr. Hanna's statement. I thoroughly agree that his thesis is correct, that our curriculum should be so designed to at least expose all of our children to a common set of values and a common fund of knowledge. I am of the opinion that a common set of values would be a crimson thread that should run through our pattern of education. If we are to be strong we must unite on common beliefs, accept a set of values, and pledge our faith to definite ideals.

Much Already Done . . .

Paul J. Reinert, President, St. Louis University

Dr. Hanna appears to present two problems:

1. To preserve democracy we need a fundamental foundation for our beliefs, a common heritage, a sort of "public philosophy."

2. We need to keep assimilating into the curriculum those new developments on the "exploding frontiers of human thought and endeavor."

Dr. Hanna seems to present this as one problem, the first one. The solution he proposes is one designed to solve the second problem.

Actually, much is already being done toward a solution of this second problem. For instance, the National Science Foundation conducts a large number of institutes for science teachers during the summer to bring them up to date on new scientific developments and teach them ways of introducing these new discoveries into the curriculum. Mathematics teachers, through similar institutes, are likewise working on revisions of the secondary school curriculum in mathematics as well as new programs in other areas.

What Dr. Hanna proposes is a further extension of this work. Such a proposal is certainly praiseworthy.

Welcome Step . . .

Charles S. Rhyne, President, American Bar Association

The value of a standard national educational curriculum, designed to encompass adequate coverage of basic areas of knowledge such as the humanities, social and physical science, and mathematics, and allowing leeway for the lesser communities to insert courses to meet specific state and local needs, cannot be denied. Just as certain basic knowledge is requisite to competent understanding of and work in the fields of law, medicine, or engineering, so familiarity with the basic arts and sciences is necessary to afford our youth the opportunity to appreciate and fulfill the role of a responsible citizen in society. Especially is this true under a republican form of government.

As with any major project there are great hurdles to be overcome, but the goal of assuring American youth of a chance to have a grounding in the fundamental areas of man's endeavor is well worth the effort. Dr. Hanna's proposal is a welcome first step in the right direction.

NOTE

1. The only exceptions would be such commissions and committees as have from time to time been created for the purpose of examining school objectives and performance. The best known of such efforts is the Educational Policies Commission of the National Education Association and the A.A.S.A.

In the following, the third reprint of this set, I attempted to refine the curriculum content required for the survival and progress of our democratic society. The paper was first delivered as an address to a 1960 workshop of the State Federation of District Boards of Education (New Jersey). It is evident that I had not yet formulated a procedure for accomplishing the desired goals.

I applaud a statement of the problem made by Abraham Lincoln: "The philosophy of the classroom in one generation will be the philosophy of government in the next." How may we assure that classroom teachers throughout our nation teach our children basic democratic values and skills? Without some universal guidance, the results of teaching and learning could be chaotic.

Educating Today's Youth— Tomorrow's Citizens*

3

The "expanding universe" (the theme of this eighth annual workshop) sits daily for its portrait. Our scientists, social scientists, and humanists are probing here, measuring there, and from these explorations we know a great deal about the potentialities and something of the realities of tomorrow.

But this tomorrow is already here for our children and youth. The mystic year 2000 is only 40 years away: children now in our elementary schools (average age 10 years) will be 50 at the turn of the century and today's secondary school pupils (average age 15 years) will be 55 at this century point. So tomorrow's citizens are being formed in our classrooms today. The implications for school curriculum are many and demanding on school boards and on the professional educators.

The first crucial question we must ask is this: shall we educate these citizens of tomorrow to (1) adjust to the changes whatever they may be, or (2) direct and control the changes to suit our values and desires? The first of these two possible answers assumes that the changes associated with the expanding universe are the result of fate or of chance—the working of forces beyond our human power to know or to command. An education appropriate to such an assumption would stress flexibility of character, a willingness to accept whatever emerges, a pragmatic outlook on life.

*Reprinted with permission, *New Jersey School Leader*, September 1960.

The second possible answer assumes that modern man, possessing a vast body of fact and principle and having acquired considerable skill in the scientific approach to problem solving, can expand the areas of control over the forces of nature; and by knowing more about individual and group behavior can create and shape our laws, institutions, and customs to achieve more of the values we hold dear. In this view of change, man becomes increasingly master of his fate rather than a puppet in fate's hands. An education geared to this assumption would stress the importance of each pupil acquiring to the limits of his capacity all of the high priority generalizations, principles, values, and competencies which will be basic to man's increasing mastery of nature and of himself. The value chart for the future citizen will consist mainly of the human rights and of the democratic ends and means which our ancestors have fashioned for us in the Golden Rule, the Declaration of Independence, the Bill of Rights, Lincoln's Gettysburg Address, and other comparable great documents from history. On the foundations of these generalities of knowledge and of the values for guiding human conduct, our children as tomorrow's citizens will build more stately mansions in their time.

But the answer is not a simple "either, or" choice between education for adjustment to change or education for directing and mastering change. Obviously both educational objectives are still valid and both will shape the kind of a curriculum we provide in our schools in this century.

To proceed with the analysis: What are some of the more challenging characteristics of the expanding universe that today's children—tomorrow's citizens—must master? One could say, "master or perish." But for the moment we will stay on the positive theme. There are seven potentially constructive phases of tomorrow about which we already know enough to project the current trends with considerable confidence:

1) The future will be known as the **power age** because we will have available mechanical power from solar and nuclear sources that will make possible almost any material task man desires.

2) The future will be known as an **age of electronics** because we will have available fantastic instruments and devices that will automatically direct and supervise mechanically powered machines to do man's work; electronic devices that will store vast quantities of information and make them instantly available to answer almost any question; electronic devices that will break down the barriers of language and make the spoken and printed word in any language understood by all other humans; and other electronic inventions that will in wondrous ways make each of us more affluent than the possessor of Aladdin's lamp.

3) The future will be known as an **age of chemistry** because man will chemically reconstitute matter to suit his special needs.

4) The future will be known as the **age of abundance** because by combining the potentials of power, electronics, and chemistry man can fashion a material world in which poverty and famine will be eliminated and each person may use as much as he needs to sustain his physical life on a high level. This abundance will be accompanied by increasing leisure time in which to live the good life. The rising expectations of oppressed peoples can be met during the lifetime of today's children.

5) The future will be known as an **age of longevity and health** because man is conquering disease, increasing the life expectancy, and generally improving the health of all.

6) The future will be known as an **age of nationhood** because within the remaining years of this century the number of communities of men seeking independence will more than double the present number of nations. The present 84 member nations in the United Nations will probably double within the next two years.

7) The future will be known as an **age of increasing interdependence** because science and technology are destroying the natural and cultural barriers that once separated mankind into an almost infinite number of isolated and insulated neighborhood, local, or state communities. The increasing interdependence can already be seen in the growth of metropolitan communities, in the importance of the emerging region-of-states community that lies between the state and the national communities, in the universal concern of nations to align themselves with other national communities, and in the developing services and significance of the United Nations as the core of an emerging world organization of nations.

So far in this discussion we have noted seven of the characteristics of the expanding society our children will inherit from us and which potentially will fulfill man's dreams of the good life. All these promises of tomorrow can be our children's joyful possessions. I say "can be"—if we teach our children the generalizations, values, and competencies essential for directing and shaping the changes now taking place.

But there are other aspects of the emerging and expanding universe that are full of danger, that could destroy much or all that we hold precious. I refer here to only two of these which, if permitted to follow their present course unchallenged and unchecked, will diminish to hollow mockery the seven positive characteristics just sketched.

1) The future could be known as the **age of overpopulation** in which the exploding population ratio of the first half of this century could strip the earth's natural resources and crowd humanity to the point where even standing room would be impossible on the earth's surface. The nearly three billion humans today could easily be doubled to six billion by 1990 and again doubled by 2200 to twelve billion—all this within the lifetime of our children in school today. The logical consequence of such a population explosion would be a struggle for survival that could destroy civilization.

2) The future could be known as the **age of the communist slave state** if the announced objectives of the world-wide party apparatus are successful in destroying the individual, and the institutions, laws, and values which freedom-loving peoples have sacrificed so much to create. The pilot projects of the Russian and Chinese communists in enslaving the Hungarians or the Tibetans stand as vividly horrifying lessons to all mankind of what could happen universally if communists were to be successful in their ruthless war for world enslavement.

We now come to the heart of this third general session: **Educating Today's Children—Tomorrow's Citizens.** What shall we teach these children of ours so that they may in their time shape those events which are within the power of intelligent and determined men and adjust to those events over which man has little or no control, and to know which events belong to each of these two broad categories?

In the first place, knowledge is already so extensive that it is impossible for any man to know everything. This problem of quantity and complexity of knowledge increases with each passing decade. We realistically must select the most important generalizations from the humanities, the social sciences, and the sciences and declare these to constitute the core of the school curriculum. Further, educators must devise psychologically sound teaching-learning experiences so that pupils may inductively arrive at generalizations in such a manner that subsequent behavior will be guided by the generalizations thus learned.

Secondly, knowledge by itself is not sufficient to master the future. We must select the values that racial experience finds to be universally true and impart these to our children and youth in such a pedagogically sound manner that conduct will be shaped by these values.

A third educational requirement is that we shall teach our young those skills and competencies required not only for individual and national continuity and survival, but also those skills we refer to as creative or scientific. The expanding universe does not yet, and probably never will, have all the answers. Our children must be taught the joy and challenge of adventure into the unknown.

All these educational goals we must strive to achieve. And what will the curriculum design be? I shall confine my discussion to four aspects of a curriculum that seems suited to the demands of the expanding universe. There is no suggestion of priority in the order of discussion: all four aspects are part of the whole curriculum design and none can be neglected.

1) We must continue to give attention to teaching the communicating skills of speaking and listening, of writing and of reading. While direct experience is the primary source of understanding, yet it is the vicarious experience of the race as recorded in language that frees man from the here and now. Schooling has always been known as a "writing and reading" institution and will always remain so.

2) Attention will continue to be paid to content, to substance, as well as to communication skills. The content of the curriculum can be conceived as having three main strands: the man-to-thing, the man-to-man, and the man-to-spirit. Another way of naming these strands, more academic perhaps: mathematics and the sciences, the social sciences, and the humanities.

No citizen of tomorrow can be individually competent nor happy without an appreciation of science and some mastery of the basic principle of the several sciences. Mathematics for tomorrow, while not limited to natural science, is essential to the operation of technology. The curriculum must systematically provide for teaching-learning of mathematics and science from the primary grades on.

3) The man-to-man relations or the social sciences become more dominant in our lives as science and technology make the human family more interdependent. Economics, political science, sociology, and particularly history and human geography have more central places in the school curriculum today than in the past. These aspects of human behavior must be studied in each of the expanding communities of men to which each of us simultaneously belongs: the family, the neighborhood, the local community, the county, the metropolitan, the state, the region of states, the nation, and the associations of nations. Each of these several communities has emerged to solve problems that lesser communities could not

handle alone. The curriculum divisions of schools are currently engaged in the social studies program in research, design, and development to provide teachers with improved social studies guides and pupil materials.

4) Man lives not by bread alone. The school curriculum must stress with equal energy the spiritual, the aesthetic, and the creative. Art, music, literature, and other muses must be a part of a complete curriculum design. This is particularly true as man's conquest of the physical and material world frees him to build a life of beauty and goodness. Our survival in the generations ahead may well depend on what our schools do today to prepare man for constructive use of abundance and leisure.

Today's children have a right to expect of us, their elders, a school curriculum that will give them the best possible preparation for individual success and happiness and for national survival and progress in a world setting. It is our moral obligation to select those generalizations, values, and competencies which seem most crucial for our survival and progress and to teach our children and youth these things. But at the same time, we must teach them that in their time they will discover new truths which will change many of the lessons we select for them today.

Curriculum planning is the central challenge to school boards and professional educators. Our task well done today may make it possible for tomorrow's citizens to avoid the threats and to achieve the potential good life which is emerging in our time.

In 1961 President Hollis Caswell of Teachers College, Columbia University, addressed the issue of curriculum reform as a part of his annual report. His forceful argument against my proposed "Design for a National Curriculum" reinforced my resolve to propose and defend a national curriculum commission. I am grateful for permission to reproduce his statement here.

CONTROL OF THE CURRICULUM
IN AMERICAN SCHOOLS*

4

An unusual circumstance has arisen in connection with the planning and control of the curriculum of American public schools.

In debates on Federal aid to education in the Congress the fear continues to be expressed very forcefully that such aid will result in diminishing the power of the states and localities to control their schools—especially in regard to the curriculum—and will inject increasing amounts of Federal control. This has been the principal argument against Federal aid through the years during which efforts have been made to secure it. If one were to consider the Congressional discussions of the subject, he would conclude that there is almost unanimous agreement that state and local control of the curriculum of American public schools is an extremely important foundation stone of our educational system.

Yet over the past few years there has been increasing evidence that some influential educators and laymen believe that national needs are minimized or ignored by states and localities in planning the curriculum. Several proposals, varying in nature but with essentially the same objective, have been made to correct this situation. While most proposals aver support for state and local control, they provide that some

---

*From the Annual Report to the Trustees, 1960–1961, Teachers College, Columbia University.

kind of national body should be established that would share in the process of curriculum planning. A permanent national curriculum council or commission is the most common suggestion.

Needless to say, these proposals are of great importance in the long-range development of American education. Our country has rigorously held that having an educational program which is controlled by the states and localities is one of its great democratic strengths. Following World War II both Germany and Japan were urged to develop local initiative and control of education. I recall attending a meeting of citizens with school authorities in a German town which was part of a plan developed by the program of school reform organized by our Office of Military Government. The people were ill at ease and there was scarcely any real give and take between the citizens and the professionals. The reason for this phase of school reform was obvious. We had seen in both of these countries how the national governments used the schools as a direct means of serving their inhuman, tyrannous ends. Hitler had the textbooks rewritten and the program of instruction arranged to advance the terrible ideas he expressed so forcefully in *Mein Kampf*. The program of instruction in the Japanese schools supported the purposes of the militarists.

At that time we were convinced that in a democracy the curriculum and instruction should be directly responsible to the will of the people served. The proposals now being made would appear to question this assumption, at least to some degree, by insisting that educational programs controlled by states and localities ignore vital national needs. This is a very serious, far-reaching matter indeed.

It is my conviction that these proposals, if accepted, would result in a significant change in the direction and control of the curriculum in American schools. It is quite unrealistic for the proponents to assert on the one hand full loyalty to the principle of state and local control and on the other the need for a national agency to correct weaknesses of this type of control.

Principal Arguments for Change

A major argument advanced in behalf of these proposals is that with modern communication and our larger role in world affairs, the development of widely accepted national purposes and the achievement of a common body of knowledge have become of overriding importance. Local school authorities are not sufficiently aware of national purposes and needs, according to this view, with the result that the curriculum has been "splintered and divided," and lacks essential common elements. It may appropriately be noted that this criticism of the curriculum was eloquently stated by Harold Rugg in the 1926 *Yearbook of the National Society for the Study of Education.*[1]

A second argument is that because our people have become highly mobile, it is essential that students be able to transfer more readily from school to school and from state to state without encountering significant differences in the curriculum. Anything which would foster a common national design, it is held, for this reason would be desirable. This is by no means a new viewpoint. William C. Bagley frequently stated it in forceful terms in his writing a quarter of a century ago.[2]

A third argument is that local school systems simply cannot command the expert competence needed to deal effectively with complex curriculum problems. A national agency, it is held, would be in position to provide local groups with plans, results of research studies, and source materials which they otherwise would not have available.

These several arguments differ in important respects, and the instrumentalities which would be set up by the various "proposers" would, in consequence, vary in function and form. However, they all have one essential point in common: **a single agency, national in scope**, would be given a preferred position of influence upon the curriculum of American schools. No longer would organizations such as the Association for Supervision and Curriculum Development, the Council of Learned Societies, the various subject-matter organizations, the Education Policies Commission, and *ad hoc* groups such as the Panel on Education of the Rockefeller Brothers Fund, Inc., and the White House Conference on Education have equal opportunity in the market place of ideas. A **national commission** staff would analyze and evaluate. Inevitably they would be in a favored position to influence practice throughout the nation.

I have examined with great care the arguments and plans for such action. Many of those making the proposals are persons of wide professional experience and high competence. Nevertheless, I have been forced to the conclusion, based on many years of study of curriculum problems and experience in curriculum work, that the establishment of any single national curriculum commission or agency would be a mistake which would very likely start America on an undesirable course of educational development. This course would, in my opinion, result in the gradual, long-range rise of centralized control of the curriculum of our schools, either unofficially through the preferred status given such an agency or legally if it were made an agency of the Federal Government. Local initiative would tend to decrease, and we would thereby, through the erosion of time, have cast out one of the great sustaining features of our educational system, that is, **its grounding in the direct concern and judgment of the mass of the people as to what is best for their children**. I cannot help believing that what is best for individual children will in the long run be best for our communities, our states, and our nation. This belief, I feel, is close to the heart of the democratic conception.

Centralization Is the Issue

Customarily, local control and Federal control are placed in opposition. Few if any persons argue for Federal control. Both major political parties take great care to make it clear that they are in favor of local control and opposed to Federal control. Most proponents of a national curriculum commission contend that the plans they propose would be free from Federal control. A self-perpetuating lay body with long, overlapping terms is one proposal. Other proposals provide different safeguards.

But the fact is that **centralization** vs. **state and local control** is the real issue. Each of the proposals involves an agency with **power**, even though it may not have a legal basis for enforcement. Imagine the situation when the **national curriculum commission** made a recommendation. It would take an extremely well-established local administrator to oppose such a recommendation with his local board of education and community. Advocates of a national commission wish to establish it because, through its exclusive role, its national stature, and the nature of its membership, its recommendations would have a special authoritative basis and its status would be particularly powerful.

The proposal to separate such a commission from the administration of education in the Federal Government through the establishment of a self-perpetuating body only makes matters worse. Such a group would have most of the influence of any specially designated national body and would be responsible to no one.

Limitation on Innovation and Experimentation

The curriculum of American schools in the past has depended substantially on the initiative and experimentation of local school systems for improvements. The result has been widely diverse practice. Proponents of a national curriculum commission decry this situation, and call for greater uniformity.

There is good reason to believe that with a single national curriculum commission such uniformity would result. Local schools would have an authoritative source upon which to rest, and so long as they followed the plans and procedures suggested by the commission, they could justify ther position before the public. They would be largely relieved of responsibility to study, to analyze, and to justify their programs in the light of local, state, and national needs. If the commission recommended study of a modern foreign language for all pupils from the third through the twelfth grade, local authorities would, in my opinion, be less inclined to inquire how it actually worked, whether it really met the needs of boys and girls, and whether there was a cultural setting in their communities which made such a move wise. They would have the authoritive recommendation to rest upon. Worse, they would tend to be suspect if they did not follow the recommendation of the commission.

If the commission recommended that all students in high school with an IQ above 110 should be required to study only the "hard academic subjects," the great majority of schools would tend to comply. There would be less inclination than under local control to give attention to the high-ability student who had great aptitude for and interest in music, art, or some other non-academic field. State and local school systems would, I believe, tend to conform to a pattern rather than to experiment and justify innovations. Even in the sequences in particular subjects this would be true. This is the result apparently sought by most advocates of such a plan.

To me, intelligent innovation and the development of improved practices are essentials of American education. I resist anything which will restrict this dynamic feature of our system.

Possibility of Control by Special Groups

Our decentralized educational system is one of the greatest safeguards we have against tyranny. No person or clique or foundation or association can easily gain control of all American education. Huey Long ran education in Louisiana, but he could not touch neighboring states. Patriotic, labor, or business associations upon occasion may succeed in getting certain books censored in the schools of one state or community, but they would have to travel a long road to control all American education. A professional association or foundation may quite readily exert great influence on education in particular states or communities, but the case must be made with hundreds of superintendents and school boards before a national movement is achieved. For example, experimental, inadequately tested programs of teaching large groups by television might have been extended to practically all American schools by now, if certain powerful forces had been in position to work through a single national curriculum commission. In years gone by we might have seen the platoon school or the contract plan become the national pattern.

A national commission on the curriculum would give such groups a ready avenue to national influence. We can be sure, I believe, that major effort would be made to control the membership of such a commission, and favored lines of development and partisan projects would be pushed vigorously for endorsement on a national basis. I feel quite sure that many current advocates of such a plan would be most unhappy if their particular approaches to curriculum development were not adopted by the commission.

This danger would be especially great if the commission were a special body initially appointed by the President but continued on a self-perpetuating basis. Responsible to no one, it would be fair game for all who wished to control the schools. Personally, I would consider a commission under the administration of the United States Commissioner of Education potentially less dangerous. At least in this case regular political channels would exist through which public opinion generally could make itself felt.

Is There Need for Greater National Conformity?

One of the basic arguments for such a commission is that we need greater national conformity in purpose and goal, and that the schools should contribute more significantly to this end. Actually, there is much sociological evidence that we have become a nation very much inclined to "keep up with the Joneses." Individuality, creative imagination, and special aptitudes are frequently smothered under uniform treatment of all pupils. There are ominous signs that many people in America are losing self-reliance because individual aptitudes and interests are too often ignored in school programs and a general culture which foster mass conformity.

This past winter an English educator who had just completed two months visiting schools in all parts of our country conferred with me at some length about major developments in American education. On this first visit to the United States he was greatly surprised by the extent of uniformity he found in American schools. He had expected from his reading to find great diversity of practice. In his view, there is much more uniformity in the curriculum of American schools than is true in

English schools. While this is the opinion of only one observer, it is unexpected and worth some consideration.

It is my opinion that the individual student is receiving all too little attention in American education at the present time. The strongest school program is one in which each child is studied and the best possible opportunities **for him** are provided. This procedure, not a national curriculum plan defined by a national curriculum commission, will give us the greatest possible assurance that we are teaching those common elements of our heritage which it is important for all to know. A study of what is good education for individuals inevitably will include what is required to make them effective citizens of our nation. If this is omitted they will experience difficulty in finding a constructive role in our social life.

It is essential, of course, that schools contribute to common national goals. In my experience local curriculum committees are more likely to be concerned with such goals than they are with the needs and conditions of the local communities they serve. It should be noted that never in our history have there been so many forces to bring national needs to the attention of the people. The President frequently speaks to the nation via television, his press conferences are televised, the same television and radio commentators are heard throughout large sections of the country, chains of newspapers carry identical editorials, popular newspaper columnists are read from coast to coast. Compare this situation with what has existed at any other time in our history. Our nation absorbed millions upon millions of immigrants during a period when it required days to get from one part of the country to another and when television and radio were unknown. Yet during those years a powerful sense of national destiny and purpose developed.

The Larger Picture

These proposals and concerns are really part of a larger picture. There is no doubt that more and more our lives have come to be controlled by centralized goverment. The basic question, I believe, is whether education will be swept into this centralizing process.

A much-discussed report of the Committee on Mission and Organization of the U.S. Office of Education helps underline this issue. While indicating in its opening sentence that the basic mission of the U.S. Office of Education will remain the same as it has been historically, the report makes it very clear that a quite different range and type of program is envisioned. The statement is made in the report that, "These new responsibilities reflect nothing more or less than a change in public conviction as to the role of the Federal Government in the area of Education." However, the views on education set forth in the Congress and by the two major political parties hardly seem to support this statement. The report further states, "It [the U.S. Office of Education] is to be reponsible for the monitoring . . . of Federal activities that affect the Nation's educational well-being. As such, it must assume the role of a voice of conscience within the Federal Government, speaking for the long-term national interest in education, in contrast to the voices that speak of a shorter-range Federal interest . . . "[3]

In fairness, it should be emphasized that the report mentions frequently that the "center of gravity" in American education should continue to rest outside the Federal Government. Even so, the general emphasis of the proposals can be interpreted only as meaning less local and more Federal control of education.

The Long-Range Trend

The problem as I see it is one of long-range trend. As a nation we can take steps to support and strengthen our tradition of local initiative and control of education or we can act so as to set in motion a trend toward centralized control. At the present time there is a decided tendency on the part of those who support particular proposals for change to consider change in itself to be progress, and to label as reactionaries those who oppose or question such plans. This attitude is unfortunate, for it defeats open examination of alternative courses of action. Certain steps which could be taken toward improvement of the curriculum would, I believe, be consistent with our tradition of local control and would serve to strengthen rather than undermine it. Such approaches merit careful study. I shall give three illustrations.

1. There can be little question about the need for much more systematic, long-range research on curriculum problems and on the development of curriculum materials. Throughout the nation there are few specialists who give their full time to such work. I would very much favor the establishment of special curriculum laboratories in from four to six major graduate schools of education which have wide national influence. These laboratories would have specific responsibility for conducting curriculum studies of the widest possible import for the schools of the nation, and could well be financed by grants similar to those provided under the National Defense Education Act. They should be assured of a minimum of five years of operating funds and should be viewed as relatively permanent additions to our educational system.

With this number of such centers at work, each associated with a university, the danger of a single dominant national commission would be avoided. No doubt conflicting results frequently would be reported. The body of reliable, carefully developed curriculum materials would increase, but state and local school systems still would have to appraise and select. Thus, the tendency toward centralized control would not be encouraged.

2. More vigorous efforts should be made to see that every local school unit has a competent and adequate curriculum and supervisory staff. Since many of our local school units cannot possibly afford adequate staffing for curriculum development and instructional supervision, plans for consolidation and reorganization should be developed and put into operation even more rapidly than at present so that every school would soon be within a soundly organized supervisory unit. The action of states in this regard is critical. Financial aid and other devices may appropriately be used to a greater extent to achieve this desirable end.

With such an organization functioning generally at the local level, many of the weaknesses about which advocates of a national curriculum commission complain would be eliminated. In fact, it is my view that this would be a far more certain approach to correction than working from the top down. It is not courses of study and syllabi which teachers need primarily as a means toward curriculum improvement; it is help in learning how to be better teachers. Anyone who has worked with curriculum programs knows how tempting it is to believe that a printed document will correct curriculum weaknesses and how generally this belief fails the test of actual practice. Good courses of study, textbooks, and reference materials will stay on the shelves gathering dust unless teachers know how to use them and wish to do so. Most teachers do the best they know how. The central problem is to help them build new and more significant understandings and skills. Thus, an effective local supervisory unit is essential.

3. I have just stressed how important I consider the competence of individual teachers is in developing an improved curriculum. The one point at which I believe a national minimum standard might desirably be established is the preparation of teachers for the various fields. If all our teachers had a good general education, sound knowledge in the fields they teach, and adequate professional preparation, there would be very much less to worry about than at present. This is in fact the crux of fundamental curriculum improvement as I see it.

We have too many teachers trying to teach mathematics who know little mathematics, or trying to teach children to write who themselves are inept at writing. We have too many teachers who follow antiquated and outworn methods, who are uninformed about materials which challenge children, and—last but not least—who are quite ignorant of the great social and personal purposes of the school as one of democracy's chief means of perpetuation. In my opinion, we need better-prepared teachers in the first place, and, in the second place, we need curriculum and supervisory programs that will help them grow constantly in competence.

A national curriculum commission, by saying in effect, to state and local school systems, "This is too complex a matter for you to undertake, let us provide you the answers," would tend to defeat this basic need for a body of professionals continuously seeking greater competence. To the extent that this happened the foundation of a school system dedicated to providing the best possible education for every boy and girl would be undermined.

A Challenge to Educational Scholarship

The problem of the control of education obviously is of very great importance. It is apparent that highly significant changes in this regard may be in the formative stage for American schools. The judgments of experienced educators such as those who are suggesting changes and the analysis here presented are of some value in determining a course of action. However, what is needed most in dealing with an issue as basic as this is the rigorous application of the knowledge and methods of study represented by related disciplines.

Specialists in comparative education, in history of education, and in educational administration—among others—should be at work on the many facets of this problem. This is precisely the kind of situation which should challenge able scholars in education. Too little systematic, rigorous research and study have been undertaken in this area. The result is that opinion clashes with opinion, and knowledge about the precise nature of the issue and possible outcomes of various courses of action is little advanced.

It is my hope that scholars from various fields on the Teachers College faculty and in other graduate schools of education will submit this critical issue to searching analysis so that the course our country takes may be based on the most adequate knowledge it is possible to achieve.

NOTES

1. Harold Rugg, "Three Decades of Mental Discipline: Curriculum Making via National Committees." *The Twenty-Sixth Yearbook of the National Society for the Study of Education* (Bloomington, Ill.: Public School Publishing Co., 1926), pp. 33–66.

2. William C. Bagley, *Education and Emergent Man* (New York: Thomas Nelson and Sons, 1934), pp. 145–46.

3. *A Federal Education Agency for the Future.* Report of the Committee on Mission and Organization of the U.S. Office of Education (Washington, D.C.: U.S. Department of Health, Education, and Welfare, 1961), pp. 4–5.

━━━━━━━━━━━━━━━━━━━━━━━━━━━━━━━━━
━━━━━━━━━━━━━━━━━━━━━━━━━━━━━━━━━

In the following article, first published in the Phi Delta Kappan *in 1961, I substantially modified my original proposal for a national curriculum (see Chapter 2). By this time I had come to see that we must avoid the possibility that a federal agency might become the creator and monitor of what is taught in schools. Such power in the hands of a totalitarian group could destroy the liberty and freedom of the individual in a democratic society. This realization led me to propose the creation of an independent National Commission for Curriculum Research and Development.*

Proposed—A National Commission for Curriculum Research and Development[*]

5

Should we have a nationwide, nongovernmental commission for curriculum research and development to provide continuing leadership in formulating educational objectives and in recommending ways to improve the school curriculum for our national community?

Several outstanding proposals have been made. In the September, 1956, issue of *The Nation's Schools*, Finis Engleman stated that "the schools of our nation need some curriculum experiences in common. . . . Some common values, some common understandings, and some common qualities must bind our people together in these times when factions from within and enemies from without would tear our nation asunder. . . . Curriculums should be designed, therefore, to develop [the] competencies required."

Earlier (May, 1945) Emeritus Professor Thomas Briggs of Teachers College, Columbia, proposed in the NASSP *Bulletin* a "curriculum commission" consisting of a "staff of the ablest . . . men and women of the nation working continuously on a full-time basis."

Within the past year or so the debate has continued. *The Nation's Schools* carried articles and editorial comment. Many journals have reported on a January, 1959, conference on the problem, held at the Center

---

*Copyright 1961, Phi Delta Kappan, Inc.

for Advanced Study in the Behavorial Sciences at Stanford. Summer workshops and conferences have furthered the analysis.

We live in a time of great expectations; we are at the same time tormented by the tensions of national and world problems. The promises and the problems have been spelled out by the President's Science Advisory Committee, by the Special Studies Project Committee of the Rockefeller Brothers Fund, by the Educational Policies Commission, by the President's Commission on National Goals, and by many more.

Modern men, using science and technology, have overloaded the ancient culture patterns inherited from our ancestors. These historic patterns are no longer able to carry the modern culture load, for at least two reasons:

1. Each prescientific society, living essentially in isolation from other societies, built an indigenous culture reflecting its conditions and desires. Customs, institutions, laws, and values emerging in each society often differed sharply from those in other societies. When one society extended its trade, influence, or boundaries, strife typically resulted. The strife continued until one or the other conquered or until conflicting customs, institutions, laws, and values had been resolved in a new culture that was indigenous to and therefore compatible with the newly combined and enlarged community.

Modern men live in another such transitional period of human history. Our modern drama takes place, however, on a much vaster stage: The whole planet is involved in a gigantic conflict of cultures.

New cultural patterns are in the making. If we move wisely and courageously, we may transform a world divided by tension and revolution into a world of justice, plenty, [truth,] peace, order [under law], and freedom.

2. There is a second sense in which ancient culture patterns are inadequate. Our ancestors lived without benefit of modern science and technology. Our forefathers did their work primarily with muscle power moving a few simple tools. Their social, economic, and political institutions, as well as their ethical values, were nicely meshed with their technics of "hunting and fishing," or of "agriculture," or of "mercantilism." The cultural balance between institutions and values on one hand and the technics available in such prescientific societies on the other gave assurance of survival and continuity.

But today's mechanically-powered, automation-directed technics throw the inherited culture patterns off balance. Our social, economic, and political endeavors lag behind achievements in the material and physical aspects of our culture. The resulting cultural imbalance causes much of our trouble.

How shall we as a nation move to restore a dynamic balance? How shall we face a future so difficult and yet so filled with promise for achieving the good life for all men? Shall we leave the future to luck and to chance? Or are there things we can do to assure victory for all mankind?

Certainly part of the solution will be found in an improved school curriculum.

The following proposal is presented with the hope that it may stimulate nationwide discussion:

> *Our desire to perpetuate and advance our cherished national values and institutions requires the creation of a non-governmental, nationwide commission for curriculum research and development.*

Such a national commission would consciously and continuously contribute to the effectiveness of education in achieving national goals. This proposal is the logical conclusion to a series of considerations which, stated briefly, are:

— A modern view of *change;*

— a modern view of *community;*

— the dual *purposes of education;*

— the soundness of the American theory and practice of *assigning responsibility for curriculum to the local and state communities;* and

— *a nationwide commission* to provide local and state school authorities with comprehensive and alternative curriculum recommendations to help develop the common school content.

Change.   The proposal as stated above involves a basic assumption about change. Life for our remote ancestors remained constant from generation to generation. Change was the exception. Permanence was the chief characteristic of man's existence.

But with the coming of enlightenment, the older crust was broken and revolutionary new ideas and events developed. Men gradually came to expect change. During this recent past, three views of change emerged:

1. Change is the result of supernatural forces entirely outside of man's knowledge or will.

2. Change is the result of chance; what happens will be the unpredictable result of actions and interactions that follow no plan, rules, or laws.

3. Change is, within limits, increasingly the result of human knowledge, choice, and action.

The first and second of these views have honorable histories. Implicit in the third, which is accepted by a growing assembly, is the belief that education can make a profound difference in achieving our national goals.

Community. In the proposal we are here considering the national community and the state and local communities are specifically mentioned. Such modifiers as "national," "state," and "local" are widely coupled with the generic term, "community." Actually, we moderns are becoming accustomed to speak of expanding communities that start with the family and extend outward like a series of concentric circles through the neighborhood community, the local community, the county community, the metropolitan community, the state community, the region-of-states community, the national community, the region or association of nations, and finally, at the outer limits, the world.

In the long sweep of human history, effectively organized communities of men larger than the local community have been the exception rather than the rule. Not until means of communication had improved to the point where people living in a larger arena could feel common ties and face and solve problems through united effort did states join with states to form nations; and still more recently nations have joined with other nations successfully in such emerging communities as the North Atlantic Treaty Organization, the Organization of American States, or in the Communist bloc. We have had centuries of time in which to build and consolidate our cultures in our state or lesser-than-state communities. The human race is still building and testing culture patterns for the national or the larger-than-national communities which have so recently been established.

Let us consider the United States for a moment. In the early 1800s, when the system of public schools was being nurtured in this young republic, we were in that stage of expanding community development when the state was struggling to come of age. One hundred and fifty years ago communication was for practical purposes limited to lung-power and letter exchange; therefore most problems were raised and solved in the neighborhood and local community arenas.

Later in the 19th century, communication inventions increasingly brought isolated peoples together in new state communities: the cultural frontiers of that day were the borders of state communities. Our Bill of Rights and federal Constitution naturally made the establishment and control of the school curriculum the responsibility of the state. The state community, in turn, delegated much of this authority to the local community. This United States pattern of local and state responsibility for the school curriculum was then the logical result of two things: the almost exclusive role the local and state communities played in the government in that period of our national history, and our fundamental belief that human ends are served better in most endeavors if the responsibility is widely spread among the people.

But such inventions as the universal news services, the postal system, the telegraph and telephone, radio and television, the automobile, train, and plane, etc., have broken through the older barriers that separated state from state. **Modern communication and transportation have made our national community a magnificent reality.**

Our educational system, formerly geared primarily to the local and state communites, must now be deliberately designed to serve as a cohesive and preserving element in the national community as well. Modern education must prepare our children and youth to function well in each of the concentric circle communities. No one of these expanding communities can be neglected without running the risk of catastrophe caused by ignorance and by conflicts in values.

Dual Purposes of Education. Education has always had two purposes: improvement of the society and development of the individual. The emphasis has shifted from place to place and from time to time. In our national life during the 19th century, public education became a primary instrument to preserve the nation's heritage and to develop the state and national communities.

With the opening of the 20th century, the second goal of education came to the fore. Moral philosophy and educational psychology not only forced the goal of individual development into focus, but almost pushed the community improvement objective off the educational stage. A perusal of almost any current educational journal or professional text demonstrates that the purpose of schooling today is expressed primarily— often exclusively—in terms of developing the individual child.

Can we afford to continue to stress one of these two equally important goals to the neglect of the other? Surely education today must attend simultaneously to both historic purposes: the improvement of society and development of the individual. The sooner these two purposes work in harmony, the better the chance of attaining the promise of tomorrow.

Local and State Responsibility for School Curriculum. The U.S. pattern of local and state control of curriculum was made partly in response to the primitive condition of technology in the early 19th century. But even if at the beginning of the last century advanced technology had made national and international communities of equal importance with local and state, many people would still insist on placing the responsibility for final policy and action in curriculum at the local and state level. Comparative education seems to support the position that democracy is best served if the control of curriculum is placed in the hands of people who are close to the sources of power—the school voters and parents in local and state communities.

It is important that this issue be clearly understood by all. There is no need for changing the existing legislative provision for local and state responsibility for school curriculum, **provided** state and local school leaders can be supplied with the best possible curriculum materials. Final choices in the curriculum should be decentralized and kept in the hands of the people.

Curriculum Designing at Local and State Levels. What has just been said about the desirability of local and state control of curriculum may sound to some as contradictory to the major proposal of this paper. But it is not inconsistent to say that educational objectives formulated by local and state authorities must serve the national community as well.

Let us examine for a moment the shortcomings of our present efforts. The typical local community spends a tiny fraction of its budget on curriculum research and development. By contrast, modern agriculture and industry spend relatively large sums on research, design, and development. The usual school pattern is to assign to a small curriculum staff attached to the central school headquarters the task of stating educational objectives, designing a curriculum, formulating a program of studies, publishing teaching guides, and selecting instructional materials. What shortcomings are inherent in this practice?

First, the range of human knowledge and values is so vast that it requires a high degree of competence to arrange a priority of generalizations for a school curriculum. Where on the staffs of most district or state education departments do we find the scholarship in all the branches of science, mathematics, social sciences, and humanities adequate to the magnitude of the job here suggested?

In the second place, the school curriculum has seriously lagged behind the rapidly expanding frontiers of human knowledge. Research by John D. McAulay[1] of Pennsylvania State University illustrates the point. McAulay studied the geographic strand of the curriculum in the public schools of the United States over a period of twenty years. He found that a decade of time elapsed between acceptance of a new geographic generalization by professional geographers and the introduction of that material into pupils' textbooks. Further, and even more disturbing, he found that two decades elapsed between the acceptance of a geographic principle by the professional geographers and the introduction of that material into the courses of study that guide instruction in this curriculum strand.

Twenty years is a long and costly time lag in a world that leaps rather than crawls into the space age. If the slow rate of school curriculum modernization found in geography from 1928 to 1948 is still representative, children in school today will have graduated from secondary schools and colleges before their courses of study have caught up with recent advances in geographic knowledge.

It is true that great efforts at curriculum modernization are currently being made. Textbooks and courses of study improve each year. Few state or local school boards, however, can possibly afford to employ on their curriculum staffs scholars in each of the disciplines of knowledge. It is difficult to imagine Centerville or Middle City employing, full time, fifteen to twenty-five outstanding scholars in mathematics, physics, chemistry, botany, zoology, astronomy, and in all the other branches of the social sciences and humanities. If Centerville and Middle City **could** afford it, and were to employ the cream of the scholars, where would Osceola State Department of Education find enough of this scarce manpower to add to its state curriculum staff? Just to speculate on the difficulty that each of the fifty states and the 50,000 local school districts would have in finding enough scholarly talent to go around, even if they could afford to do so, should demonstrate that it is impossible for each local and state school system to maintain a complete staff of scholars for curriculum research, design, and development. It would also be a duplication of effort that neither this nation nor any other could afford.

Again we ask, how shall we satisfy the national need for an adequate education? How shall we strengthen the school curriculum to assure the common learnings of generalization, value, and competency needed by our national community? The solution here proposed is to create a **national commission for curriculum research and development**.

One must immediately acknowledge that excellent curriculum research and development are under way in many quarters. The Educational Policies Commission from time to time has produced excellent documents on the purposes of education and on the curriculum of the schools. Many educational associations and many *ad hoc* educational groups have also made proposals concerning the common learnings for the nation. The NEA Project on the Instructional Program of the Public Schools plans to issue several publications before ending its work in August, 1962.

During the 19th century, scholars in the humanities, mathematics, the social sciences, and the natural sciences gave much attention to the content of the elementary and secondary school curriculum. During the 20th century, however, the scholars have largely ignored presentation of content from their disciplines in the lower schools. But within the last decade these scholars have been turning again to the problems of elementary and secondary school curriculum. Currently, physical science scholars at the Massachusetts Institute of Technology and mathematicians at several universities are working to improve the high-school program. Several proposals are now in the formative stages: The American Council of Learned Societies proposes a study in economics and the National Science Foundation is studying the biological sciences. These organizations, and others, are hoping to improve the school curriculum.

With a different approach but with a similar motive, laymen are today more active than they have ever been in examining the school curriculum and proposing improvement and reform. The recent White House Conference on Education was a stupendous effort led by the lay segment of the national community to analyze and improve schools. The excellent statements by the Special Studies Project Committee of the Rockefeller Brothers Fund and by the President's Science Advisory Committee are examples of what laymen can do to suggest ways of strengthening the curriculum. The National Citizens Council for Better Schools organized 18,000 local groups working for improved education. The National School Boards Association is deeply concerned with the problem of curriculum. State and local school boards seek to improve those aspects of the curriculum which relate directly to national welfare. The American Textbook Publishers Institute and similar organizations are studying the place that instructional materials should have in the curriculum. And finally, the schoolman has not only a very great interest in the curriculum but an obligation to see that our children are exposed to the very best education.

But in each such effort certain inadequacies exist:

— The body has not been sufficiently broad enough to represent all the partners of the entire national community;

— the body has not had a permanent or even a prolonged existence;

— the body does not have continuous working sessions;

— the body only occasionally tackles the problem of national welfare and school curriculum; or

— the body concentrates on one strand or discipline of the curriculum at a time and makes little contribution to over-all balance of objectives in the curriculum design.

We need a permanent nationwide commission on curriculum, non-governmental, widely representative, and continuously at work on educational goals and balanced curriculum design.

We will examine a series of questions that are asked about such a commission.

What Would a National Commission Do?

We visualize that a national commission for curriculum research and development would continuously:

— Research, formulate, and reformulate the basic purposes of education for our national community in a world setting. Such a set of objectives would help assure the perpetuation and better achievement of the Bill of Rights, the values on which our way of life is built, and the great generalizations in the humanities, social sciences, and sciences drawn from the pages of history.

— Research and formulate alternative curriculum models to provide the teaching-learning experiences through which children would come to understand, appreciate, and have loyalty to our national values, laws, and institutions.

— Research systematically all the expanding horizons of man's mind and spirit and abstract therefrom those values, generalizations, and competencies that are of vital interest to the survival and progress of our national community.

— Interpret these new ideas from all the academic disciplines and make the appropriate ones available to all concerned with curriculum development.

— Emphasize the need to keep in balance the second purpose of education—development of the individual.

There is concern in some quarters that the recommendations of such a national commission could be damaging to discussion in schools of the wide variety of views held by people in a democratic society. There are those who believe schools should discourage any discussion that raises questions concerning historic or popularly accepted positions on controversial issues. But if a closed position were taken by a national commission, the result could be disastrous to a nation that needs to explore every issue and every point of view.

We believe that one of the major contributions of the proposed commission should be the clear identification of the divergent ways of viewing important problems and the encouragement of provisions in the school curriculum for study and discussion of a wide range of views. The job of the national commission would be to encourage and facilitate the creative genius of a democratic society.

Who Should Hold Membership on a National Commission?

As suggested earlier, such a commission should have on its staff outstanding persons from three segments of our national life: **scholars, laymen, and schoolmen**. This trio is a *sine qua non* to this proposal. No curriculum effort will be comprehensive enough to meet the demands of this age unless all three partners—the scholar, the layman, and the schoolman—join efforts.

The **scholars**—persons possessing special knowledge in any branch of learning—must indicate what values and concepts from the past and present seem to them to be most important and then suggest priorities.

These scholars not only study the past and analyze the present, they also scout the future. They must point out the possible directions future change may take, suggest what seem to them to be the best of the alternative directions for change, and point out the pros and cons of each alternative.

The **laymen**—persons not primarily scholars nor members of the schoolmen's profession—have the special responsibility of evaluating the priority lists prepared by the scholars and of indicating those that seem to them to be of greatest significance. In a democratic society, the citizens must finally make this choice. True, the scholars and the schoolmen are also citizens and together the choices are laid out for the curriculum designers at the local and state levels. The laymen, particularly those with school board experience, must be represented on the national commission to assure that the work of this body does not lose touch with the citizens with whom the local and state curriculum decision rests.

The **schoolmen**—persons who teach in or administer schools—must be working members of the trio. They possess the special knowledge of how a curriculum design may be constructed to take full advantage of the scholar's knowledge and of the laymen's choices and at the same time take account of modern insight into child growth and learning motivation. The schoolmen are the curriculum architects and must be working partners in the commission.

Unfortunately, in curriculum research and development to date there has been no such national joint effort of scholar, layman, and schoolman. One unique feature of this proposed national commission is that it will have built into it competent representation from each of these three segments of our society. Such teamwork is necessary for its success.

How Could Continuity for the Commission Be Provided?

The commission should have a permanent endowment or a fund sufficient to assure operation for at least a ten-year period. This endowment might come from several sources: individual or corporate donors and foundations; lay, scholarly, and professional educational organizations. There are probably other sources of funds.

In order to provide continuity in personnel, it is proposed that the commission have a small permanent staff, headed by an executive secretary. This is the way in which many professional and industrial organizations have solved the continuity problem. To this staff several of America's outstandingly visible scholars, laymen, and schoolmen should be appointed for long terms to serve full-time.

For very brief periods of time (a few weeks to a year), added specialists or generalists could be recruited from among scholars, laymen, and schoolmen to serve as consultants to do specific tasks calling for short and intensive periods of work. On such short-term appointments might be publishers and producers of instructional materials; foundation personnel seeking coordination of their programs; representatives of learned societies planning intensive curriculum work in one discipline; educational association executives planning yearbooks on curriculum; accreditation agency representatives; etc.

Thus continuity of the commission could be assured through a small permanent staff with the authority and resources to surround itself with added personnel as the evolving projects of research and synthesis develop.

What Might Be the Commission's Relationship to Other National Efforts in Curriculum?

A national commission for curriculum research and development is conceived of as a national resource, supplementing and supporting the many efforts now under way or under consideration to improve the school curriculum. Under no circumstances would this proposed commission take over or attempt to direct the well-defined curriculum projects of others. Rather than competing, this proposed commission would try at all times to understand and relate the objectives and procedures of other groups to the total curriculum undertaking. And in turn other groups or bodies concerned with curriculum should seek in the work of the national commission suggestions and support for the enhancement of their work.

In the membership of the proposed commission there would undoubtedly be individuals familiar with or intimately associated with the more specific curriculum research and development projects of the several departments of the NEA and especially of the Project on the Instructional Program of the Public Schools. Also there should be representation from the National Congress of Parents and Teachers, the American Council of Learned Societies, the National Science Foundation, and so on. Through such overlapping of personnel on the commission and other groups, the efforts of the several bodies working on the segments of the school curriculum could be informally coordinated. Through such collaboration the findings and recommendations of the several bodies could find more complete synthesis in the deliberations of the national commission.

What Authority Would a National Commission Have?

Deeply imbedded in the American character is a belief in and emotional commitment to local autonomy in school affairs. At the same time, there is a growing awareness of the chaos in school curriculum resulting from local option. There seems to be a ground swell of support for strengthening the school curriculum as a bulwark of the national community at this time when internal and external forces challenge us.

Some advocate a strong United States Office of Education to provide leadership in curriculum improvement. Congress may assume greater responsibility for curriculum guidance. The federal government for years has played a significant role in vocational education and the new National Defense Education Act takes the government into new curriculum areas.

The possibility that local and state autonomy for school curriculum may be further modified by federal participation disturbs most laymen, scholars, and educators. This possibility causes many to reject the proposal for any kind of a national commission for curriculum. They ask how one can be certain that a national commission will not become the instrument through which citizens and teachers would be denied local or state control of curriculum choices.

It is clear that this basic question must be answered to the satisfaction of the American people and the teaching profession. But if one agrees that we need a strengthening of curriculum to assure the promise of our national community, then ways can be found to achieve it. The national commission here proposed is one such solution that needs wide discussion.

The articles of incorporation of the proposed commission would have to safeguard against the commission's exerting legal control over any local or state educational body. **The commission must be advisory**. It should not have administrative mechanisms for enforcing its proposals; it must be denied power to interfere with the duly constituted bodies that have the responsibility for our school curriculum.

To answer the question more constructively, the commission would possess such influence as the logic and persuasiveness of its proposals would merit among the individuals and groups that might decide to pay some attention to its research and proposals. The commission's impact would be the result entirely of the quality of its deliberations.

In somewhat the same unofficial manner in which the nongovernmental Council on Medical Education of the American Medical Association or the independent National Safety Council both provide stimulation and leadership in their spheres of interest, so the proposed National Commission for Curriculum Research and Devlopment would stand or fall on the merits of the curriculum proposals it makes over the years.

Recently, O. H. Roberts, Jr., former president of the National School Boards Association, said that no national commission serving voluntarily in this advisory capacity can or will impose its opinions on the traditionally independent local or state school boards. He said further that he believes lay boards feel inadequate in their knowledge and judgment and would welcome the recommendations of a good commission to gain better perspective and understanding on which their decisions could be made.

The above discussion of authority, however, does not solve the basic problem for some observers. They ask, how shall the national community protect its interests against the refusal of the few to include in their curricula appropriate teaching-learning experiences that will contribute the common core of understanding and behavior so crucial to our national survival and progress? Admittedly, the proposed national commission is not a panacea. There is no guarantee that all or even most schools will take advantage of the commission's work

If adopted, however, this proposal would result in speeding curriculum advance in most schools across the nation. It would lessen the pressure for federal action at the field level. Is it not wiser to take a positive but voluntary step in the right direction and thereby preserve freedom of local and state choice? We face, one must remember, several alternatives, none of which is wholly satisfactory. The case has been stated clearly by John H. Fischer, formerly superintendent of schools in Baltimore and now dean of Teachers College, Columbia, who recently said:

> There is growing awareness of the need to improve American education, particularly the common core of the curriculum. Three alternatives have been proposed. The first is a federal educational system, which is *wholly unacceptable*. The second is to get along with the present structure and procedures, and this, too, is *inadequate* to meet the needs. The third is to maintain the present educational structure but to get national leadership for guidance in making wise curriculum decisions. This leadership would include (1) study groups to give help on the design and content of the specific strands of the curriculum and on instructional materials and procedures, and (2) a commission to deal with priorities and overriding needs. This third course of action, the establishment of a national curriculum commission, seems *most* likely to succeed.

Who Might Use the Results of the Commission's Work?

One could anticipate that the commission's periodically published educational objectives and its alternative recommendations on means of accomplishment would be a fruitful resource for study by and an inspiration to:

— Local boards of education and their professional staffs who would be completely free to ignore, reject, adapt, or adopt the commission's suggestions.

— Local Parent-Teacher Associations and other interested lay groups (AAUW, League of Women Voters, service clubs, etc.) who seek materials and guidance in their study of the curriculum.

— State boards of education and their professional staffs who, again, would be completely free to take or leave the commission's suggestions.

— State associations of school board members, educational committees of state associations of labor, business, veterans, etc., who desire help in viewing the curriculum comprehensively.

— National lay, scholarly, and educational groups who may wish to see how their particular set of interests fits into the total possibility for curriculum.

— Teacher education groups, accreditation bodies, and institutions interested in evaluating their teacher education programs.

These groups by no means exhaust the list of potential users. The current situation discloses an absence of any continuous study and pronouncement by a body of high national visibility that represents all the partners in the national education enterprise. A vast audience awaits the comprehensive help which such a commission as is here proposed could provide.

How Would Members of a National Commission Be Selected?

There are some who favor the creation of a permanent and nongovernmental national commission on curriculum research and development but suggest that its success would be affected by the composition of the commission. Who would name the members? This is a difficult hurdle. Several approaches to naming the commission members have been advanced.

Some educators believe the National Education Association should determine the composition of the commission and name its members. This has one major weakness: lay and scholarly groups want equal voice in selecting members to represent them. Just as schoolmen would not be enthusiastic about a national commission named by the scholars alone or by the laymen alone, so these laymen and scholars react to schoolmen [alone] making the decisions.

Others would have potential donors of funds name the commission members. But there is always question of the ability of donors sufficiently to divest themselves of self-interest to make an acceptable decision on this crucial matter.

Others favor an *ad hoc* group to draw up the plans for selecting commission members. This *ad hoc* group might consist of the executive secretaries of such organizations as the American Association for the Advancement of Science, the National Council of Learned Societies, the National Education Association, and the National School Boards Association.

This small group of executives could easily get together to lay down the principles of commission composition, decide on the best means of selecting the initial staff, and suggest the mechanism for filling subsequent vacancies. Once these matters had been agreed upon, their recommendations could be referred to the several interested organizations and to potential donors for study and action.

In summary, let us return to the series of considerations with which this paper opened. It is contended that:

— because we live in a dynamic era of profound change which we believe we can, with widening limits, shape to our desire and will;

— because the local and the state educational authorities are now and should remain in final control of curriculum choices and programs;

— because modern science and technology have united local and state communities in a great national community, the preservation and improvement of which makes certain demands on school curriculum;

— because few if any local or state systems of education can attract or can afford the rare talent required continuously to study and to propose priority of objectives and alternative curriculum designs that will specifically serve the national interests; and

— because the national community has no recognized and comprehensive body responsible for continuous study of educational objectives and for making the [alternative] curriculum recommendations necessary to our continuing national progress;

therefore, it follows that we should engage in nationwide discussion of how best to accomplish the desired curriculum improvements.

Note

1. John D. McAulay, "Trends in Elementary School Geography" (Unpublished doctoral dissertation, Stanford University, 1948).

I was invited to prepare the sixth reprint in this set for the 1962 NEA convention in Denver. In my remarks I expanded the proposal for a National Commission for Curriculum Research and Development. In 1959, the NEA leadership had launched a new enterprise called the Project on Instruction, in which a curriculum and instruction center was conceived as the mechanism to improve the curriculum. Although NEA officials primarily rejected the notion of a national curriculum, originally presented in 1958, many leaders responded with interest in 1962 to the concept of a National Commission for Curriculum Research and Development.

This reprint duplicates many of the points made in the previous chapters. Inasmuch as I was, for the first time, proposing an action program for the assembled NEA members (who might not have heard the earlier rationale for the proposal), I felt it necessary to present the case again in some detail.

THE NEA'S FUTURE ROLE IN CURRICULUM AND INSTRUCTION*

6

During the 1959 NEA Annual Convention at St. Louis, only three years ago this summer, our NEA leadership officiated at the birth of this Project on Instruction. The exact history of the inception and incubation of this pedagogical infant may never fully be recorded, but on this third birthday, all of us take parental and kinship pride in the husky and lusty enterprise whose report card we review today. The "happy birthday" messages have been genuine in their approbation. The National Committee and the Project Staff deserve our gratitude for their dedication and skill in guiding this educational prodigy so successfully.

The kinship group here assembled is asked to counsel this young project. We are asked to suggest possible and desirable directions for the future. The proposals we have heard here demonstrate that there is much yet to be done and that wise choices must be made to focus energy so that it not be wasted on tasks of lesser priority.

The Curriculum Challenge of the 21st Century

The youngsters in our schools today will, 38 years from now at the opening of the 21st century, be in their middle years. These citizens of

---

*From remarks to the NEA Convention, Denver, July 5, 1962.

the next century will live in a society that has either fallen into perdition or has miraculously improved man's condition.

No matter which opposed set of events one may predict, we have no choice but to work to bring about man's noblest dream of the good life.

Our advance scouting parties are out on the new frontiers, inventorying the 21st century, and reporting back to us the magnificent landscapes that lie over the horizon of the next four decades. But they also warn us of the perils and hardships that we must overcome to reach the promised land.

Our future-viewers speak of promise: of a world free from most diseases; of a life-expectancy of 100 years; of a world blessed with material abundance; of a world in which material matters will be handled primarily by mechanical energy and automation, leaving man free time in which to develop his mind and his spirit to their fullest potential. They speak of a world at peace; a world in which freedom, justice, and hope may prevail because men will have learned of their worth and the processes by which such conditions are maintained.

Who are these scouts of tomorrow? Their number is legion. These scouts are our poets, novelists, essayists, philosophers, and spiritual leaders. They are our theorists and researchers in the physical and biological sciences. They are our economists, our political scientists, our students of society. They are our logicians, mathematicians, and statisticians. They are our engineers, our agriculturists, our space men, our industrialists, our commercial leaders, and our financiers. Our pioneer scouts include these and many more who labor on the frontiers of the next century and whose reports fill us with great expectations.

But these scouts also report hardships and warn of catastrophes which might prevent us from possessing the land of milk and honey. Over-population could seriously deplete irreplaceable resources. Nuclear, biological, and chemical technology in the hands of anarchistic nations could destroy a world divided against itself. Power-hungry and fanatical dictators of the extreme left or extreme right could enslave mankind, wipe out the self-directing individual, and replace him with the faceless and nameless human cog in the state's machinery. Or the scouts report that peoples who have lived in economic or political bondage might revolt so violently that they could set back the clock of history a century or more.

These scouts of tomorrow have an irrevocable responsibility to make certain that the hopes and the anticipated frustrations of the 21st century are made known to youth now in our schools. Today's children, tomorrow's citizens, must be equipped with the values, the knowledge, and the abilities that seem most crucial for survival and progress in the decades ahead. This in brief is the challenge to curriculum.

Curriculum Designing—A Shared Responsibility

But what design or plan shall be made for selecting from among the vast cultural capital accumulated over the ages and so explosively multiplying in our new age of science? Shall we leave the designing of content to the child or youth who, out of ignorance or immaturity is as likely to learn the trivial as to master the significant? Shall we leave the design of content to the individual teacher who at best is knowledgeable about only one or two short chapters of the scouts' reports? Shall we leave the design of content to the organized teaching profession, which because of the demands of imparting knowledge and of motivating growth in youth has little energy left to join the parties scouting the frontiers of man's mind and spirit?

All of these—the learner, the learner's teacher, and teachers' organizations—have a role to play in creating the design by which content of greatest promise may be selected and taught. But in our society we deny the right of decision monopoly to any one segment of the community. The profession of teachers must never make the fatal error of assigning exclusively or even primarily to itself the task of setting forth the goals of society, determining the objectives of education, or of arranging the priority of values, generalizations, and competencies essential for survival and progress of our society. These tasks are shared in our society by at least two other groups.

The community of scholars shares with the teaching profession the responsibility of stating our goals and of content designing. Scholars in the humanities, the natural and social sciences, and in mathematics and logic have as their special contribution the discovery of new knowledge, the structuring and restructuring of knowledge, and the transmission of the processes of discovery and ordering of their disciplines. The scholars are both preservers of cultural capital and discoverers and organizers of the culture content that is yet to come. No school can possibly design an adequate curriculum without intimate and continuous partnership of the teacher and of the scholar. The NEA Project on Instruction has correctly put its roots down into the subsoil of content as organized by the community of scholars.

But a third community—laymen—likewise has a shared curriculum responsibility. In a free society, where democratic ideals are guarded and guided through representative government, the public has the final decision on what it wishes the schools to teach the young. The layman expects to share with the scholar and with the schoolman the review of societal goals and the designing of appropriate content by which our dreams and desires may become realities in the decades ahead.

The Traditional Practice of Local and State Control of the Curriculum Is Valid Today

So far I have spoken only of the curricular challenges found in the promises of tomorrow and of the shared responsibility of curriculum designing by laymen, scholars, and schoolmen to facilitate societal goals. There is a conversation heard across the nation that centers on local versus national control of curriculum and instruction. For a very few minutes I want to join in this conversation.

Local control of education is a powerful apparatus that encourages the widest possible participation of citizens and the profession of teachers in the decisions that vitally influence the content and process of schooling. If representative democracy in the United States has one condition most responsible for our successes, it is probably the historic practice of involving as many as possible of those to be affected by educational policy, in deciding what shall be taught and by what means. **State and local responsibility of schools in this nation has been and is a defensible instrument for gaining consensus on goals and policies of the several states and their numerous local communities, and for carrying out the decisions reached by these bodies**.

Local and State Communities Are Not Self-Sufficient in Curriculum

I contend that local and state school control has been and is still valid, but I must join those who question whether the local and the state school authorities are or can be self-sufficient in curriculum designing in the years ahead. It seems to me the central issue is how shall those responsible for state and local schools be sure they have before them the most significant options of educational objectives and procedures, the most rational and comprehensive and balanced curriculum designs from which to make choices suitable for their local situations.

Many voices raise searching questions about the content of the school curriculum. Among the questions, these stand out:

In a world as troubled as ours, do we not have to agree that a curriculum must at least expose all children in our nation to a common and minimum set of values and to a common fund of knowledge and skills?

Can our precious liberties and the right of the individual to be different be protected by a people whose education may not have prepared each of them to hold in common a belief in such ideals?

Can a curriculum researched and conceived primarily by the state authority and/or the local school district and administered typically by the individual teacher provide adequate foundations for the nation's unity, strength, and welfare?

Can we hope in a divided world to survive as a free people unless our enculturation includes the most significant generalizations, values, and processes drawn from the frontiers of knowledge?

These are questions pointedly asked by laymen, scholars, and schoolmen; questions for which suitable answers must be found.

Few states and relatively fewer local communities possess or can afford to assemble the rare and costly resources (personnel) necessary for continuous research into such questions as raised above. Few local and state governments can assign qualified people to full-time curriculum research, design, and development. The very survival of our nation and of free men everywhere demands that our schools throughout the nation present teaching-learning experiences that guarantee today's youth—tomorrow's citizens—will be taught and have the opportunity and encouragement to learn the highest priority understandings, values, and competencies essential to win the war being waged against free men by both communist and fascist forces. But even were we not threatened enslavement by totalitarian values and institutions, we need to make as certain as possible in a changing world, that we provide both the content and the process which will most likely preserve our democratic values and attain the vast possibilities we see on the horizon.

Our national goals in a world setting must be examined continuously, translated into educational objectives, balanced for comprehensiveness and cruciality, and embodied in **alternative** curriculum designs. Such curriculum designing requires a national and joint effort of laymen, academic scholars, and professional school personnel. During any calendar year there are usually several national projects initiated by groups of scholars to provide schools with curriculum guides and instructional materials. Currently national associations of mathematicians, of foreign language teachers, of physical or biological scientists, or economists or geographers, etc., with financial assistance from government or foundations, are providing such leadership in their respective subject matter disciplines. Simultaneously there are several national, regional, or state efforts initiated by associations of professional school people to improve the curriculum. Unfortunately, few of these efforts are conceived as an integral part of the planning for achieving national goals, nor do any of these sporadic and uncoordinated efforts have a life expectancy of more than a few years.

We need a **nation-wide commission**, or a council, or an academy that is **non-governmental** and has **no power except the force of its rational proposals for curriculum**. We need such a nation-wide body that will continuously provide the state and local lay boards and professional staffs with the best, the most comprehensive and carefully balanced sets of educational goals that are related to our national purpose, and arranged in alternative curricular designs through the use of which the goals may be approached.

But again we emphasize that the state and local school authorities must remain legally and effectively responsible for the final choices of curriculum to be used in their respective communities. Obviously, only the state and the local school authorities can know the educational needs of the state and local communities, and provide for these. But the local and the state authorities possessing the optional curriculum designs furnished by a national curriculum commission, would be helped to make wiser choices of content and method required for the national welfare than is now possible.

I believe that a national, non-governmental commission should be created to insure that those in control of schools at the local and state levels will have in their hands the richest and most comprehensive, but **optional** models of curriculum to assist them in making their local decisions. With such national help, there is every reason to believe that wise curriculum choices by local and state authorities will insure our school investment both in our youth and in the future of our nation. The theory and practice of local and state control of curriculum is still valid but requires services not practical within these less-than-national communities.

The NEA's Future Role in Curriculum and Instruction

If one accepts the basic assumptions and the logical implications of what has been said, then certain suggestions are probably in order. I make the following suggestions with full recognition that some will challenge the assumptions and that others will question the logic of the suggestions. But our profession is a mature one and profits from discussion of differing diagnoses and prescriptions.

1. The people of this nation expect the NEA to be concerned fully as much with the preservation and development of the national community as with the growth and guidance of the individual. For many of us, our focus has been primarily on education as consumption—a response to the demands of the child and youth as consumers. Our literature on curriculum and instruction is dominated with phrases that refer to the child while at the same time the literature understresses investment in the creation of cultural capital through human resource development. As the all-encompassing educational organization in this nation, the NEA should direct proper shares of its energy both (1) to curriculum research, design, and development that facilitate the national goals, and (2) to releasing and nurturing the creative potential in each and every child and youth. Not one **or** the other, but **both** objectives should be the business of the NEA. I believe the NEA should immediately take steps to create a new Curriculum and Instruction Center. The NEA should seek outside funds as well as commit a substantial portion of its own resources to finance this most significant enterprise.

2. The proposed NEA Curriculum and Instruction Center should exert strong and continuous leadership but work closely with the several departments and associations of the NEA to plan jointly for the over-all curriculum research, design, and development that will contribute directly to achieving national goals.

3. The new Center should exert leadership in aiding national groups of educators to undertake studies of separate strands of the total curriculum and further provide mechanisms through which local and state school authorities ultimately might consider whether and how such separate curriculum findings might be assimilated into or replace existing programs.

4. The three suggestions just stated have important conditions that should be made clear in every policy statement and action of the proposed new Center. If it is agreed that curriculum decisions particularly, and to a considerable extent also instruction, are the joint responsibility of the three great partners (the laymen, the academic scholars, and the professional school people), then it should follow that no one of the partners should assign itself the directing role. This matter is often highly charged with enough emotion to make good cooperative relations among the partners almost impossible. We professional school people generally resent the unilateral attempt on the part of a special discipline group to remake a subject of the school curriculum. We rightly feel we have a deep and vested interest in decisions of what content is to be taught, when, and how. Or when a lay legislative group alone attempts to de-

sign school curriculum, we feel threatened and even jealous of our prerogative.

Is it not understandable that our partners, the laymen and the academic scholars, similarly resent us when we professional school people pre-empt curriculum making to ourselves? Is it not natural that the other partners do not wish to be invited to the curriculum conference table by educators for the purpose of working on the educators' program and giving approval to assumptions and decisions which we school people have made unilaterally?

I am trying to make a point on which there will be much disagreement within our teaching profession. But I believe this new Center would be ill-advised to take unto itself the authorship and directing role of curriculum, research, design, and development and then, with purposes and ground rules tentatively agreed upon, to invite participation by the communities of scholars and of laymen.

Rather than this "you join our club" approach to the partners, would it not be more statesmanlike for the Center, without a hidden agenda in its pocket, to raise this question with national associations of scholars and laymen: How might all of us who are interested in and who possess among us the several essential components for the task, join forces? How shall we come together to work on the common cause and the appropriate mechanisms and how shall we severally conceive our distinctive but complementary roles?

I am not saying that the NEA should wait for the community of scholars and the community of laymen to initiate cooperative curriculum study. The proposed new Center, representing as it would the entire teaching profession, should seek out those scholarly and lay organizations that have responsibility and indispensable contributions to make to curriculum research, design, and development and so to approach these organizations that from the beginning a true partnership would operate. Because we school people are in the business of educating the nation's youth, it is quite natural to expect that such a consortium would mandate to the professional educators the technical work of curriculum making and instructional planning. But such use of our expertise in curriculum and instruction would be harnessed to goals agreed upon by all who claim a stake in educational planning to promote national purposes.

I would hope that the new NEA Curriculum and Instructional Center in joint action with laymen and scholars would be instrumental in forming some type of nation-wide academy, or committee, or institute, or commission whose membership would reflect the best minds and spirits of the three communities—laymen, scholars, and professional schoolmen.

It is fervently hoped that such a National Commission for Curriculum Research, Design, and Development would be non-governmental, of high national visibility, well financed, and permanently and continuously at work translating national goals into educational objectives and a balanced curriculum design. The relationship between such a National Commission and the proposed NEA Curriculum and Instruction Center should be the agenda for many work sessions among the several partners.

5. The new NEA Center should work closely with universities and colleges to study the problem of preparing teachers competent in both subject matter and instructional techniques. The curriculum challenge of the 21st century will demand a classroom teacher thoroughly familiar with the structures of knowledge and with the processes by which disciplines discover new knowledge and incorporate it into existing structures. This teacher of future citizens of the 21st century will need much more general and special knowledge and competence than is typical of the graduates of teacher preparation programs of the moment. The NEA Center should work at this task cooperatively with higher education.

6. The new NEA Center should work with educational administrative groups and lay boards of education to enhance the provision for continuous in-service growth of the teaching corps who cannot depend alone on what they previously learned in college. Obsolescence is a characteristic of every trade and profession in this rapidly changing period. The teaching profession cannot stand still with old content and method if we take seriously the curriculum challenges of the 21st century.

These few suggestions for the future role of the NEA in curriculum and instruction by no means cover the topic exhaustively. Hopefully, these suggestions are among the considerations that should govern the early efforts of our proposed NEA Curriculum and Instructional Center. With success in these early efforts, there will come new visions of the challenge and new answers to which subsequent birthday gatherings of this group will direct their counseling skills.

The following reprint is an article requested by the editor of the NEA Journal *who suggested that I summarize the ideas found in two earlier sources: the* Phi Delta Kappan *magazine article (Chapter 5) and the address to the delegates of the 1962 annual NEA convention (Chapter 6).*

For the reader who has already noted the texts of these previous chapters, there is a redundancy that is useful in following the history of the fate of the basic plan I was evolving.

One may ask why the NEA did not fully develop its proposed Project on Instruction, the main theme of the 1962 convention in Denver. Since 1927, as a young member of the NEA, I had been inspired and educated by attending the annual and regional conventions of the organization. I read the journals and brochures, and still recall today the preponderance of excellent addresses and articles on curriculum and instruction. In the 1960s, the content of the publications and conventions changed. NEA swung its focus from curriculum and instruction to a union's concern about work conditions, tenure, and compensation for its members. While such union goals are important, there remained little time and energy to pursue the original professional goals of the organization. It is interesting to note that today the Journal *of the American Federation of Teachers currently carries more seminal articles on the philosophy of education, curriculum, and instruction than does the comparable NEA publication.*

CURRICULUM AND INSTRUCTION: A PROPOSAL CONCERNING THE NEA's FUTURE ROLE IN THESE AREAS*

7

The NEA Project on Instruction is now three years old. The proposals for future Project activities which were made at the 1962 NEA convention demonstrate that there is much yet to be done and that wise choices must be made in order to focus efforts on tasks of high priority.

The youngsters in our schools today will be in their middle years at the opening of the twenty-first century. These citizens of the next century will live in a society that has either fallen into perdition or has miraculously improved man's condition. No matter which opposed set of events one may predict, we have no choice but to work to bring about man's dream of the good life.

Today's children, tomorrow's citizens, must be equipped with the values, the knowledge, and the abilities that are crucial for survival and progress in the decades ahead. This in brief is the challenge to curriculum.

What design or plan can be used to select curriculum content from among the vast cultural capital accumulated over the ages and so rapidly multiplying in our new age of science?

The learner, the teacher and the teachers' organization each has a role to play in creating the design by which the most promising content may be selected and taught. But in our society we do not allow any one segment of society to have a monopoly on decision making. The teach-

---

*From *NEA Journal: Journal of the National Education Association*, January 1963.

ing profession, therefore, must never make the fatal error of assigning exclusively or even primarily to itself the task of setting forth the goals of society, determining educational objectives, or arranging the priority of values and competencies essential for America's survival and progress. These tasks are shared by at least two other groups.

The community of scholars shares with the teaching profession the responsibility of stating our goals and of designing content. Scholars in the humanities, in the natural and social sciences, and in mathematics and logic have as their special contribution the discovery of new knowledge, the structuring and restructuring of knowledge, and the transmission of the processes of discovery.

No school can possibly design an adequate curriculum without an intimate and continuous partnership of the teacher and the academic scholar. The NEA Project on Instruction has correctly sought the wisdom of the community of scholars.

But a third community—the public—likewise has a shared curriculum responsibility. In a free society, where democratic ideals are guarded and guided through representative government, the public has the final decision on what the schools will teach the young. The layman expects to share with the scholar and with the schoolman the task of reviewing societal goals and of designing curricula which will enable our aspirations to become realities.

Having touched on the curriculum challenges found in the promises of tomorrow and on the shared responsibility for curriculum designing, let us turn to the question of local versus national control of curriculum and instruction—a question which is being raised with increasing frequency.

Local control of education is a powerful apparatus that encourages the widest possible participation of citizens and educators in the decisions that vitally influence the content and methods of education. This historic practice has been an important factor in the success of representative democracy in the United States. State and local control of schools in this nation has been and is a defensible instrument for gaining general consensus on goals and policies of education from the several states and their numerous local communities, and for carrying out the decisions reached by these bodies.

While I believe that local school control has been and is still valid, I must join those who question whether the local and the state school authorities can be self-sufficient in curriculum designing in the years ahead. The central issue, it seems to me, is how those responsible for state and local schools can be sure they have before them the most significant alternatives among educational objectives and procedures and the most rational, comprehensive, and balanced curriculum designs from which to select those suitable for their local situations.

Among the searching questions being asked about the content of school curriculum, these stand out:

In a world as troubled as ours, must we not agree on a curriculum that will at least expose all children in our nation to a common, minimum set of values and to a common fund of knowledge and skills?

Can our precious liberties and the right of the individual to be different be protected by a people whose education may not have prepared them to hold in common a belief in such ideals?

Can a curriculum researched and conceived primarily by the state authority and/or the local school district and administered typically by the individual teacher provide adequate foundations for the nation's unity, strength, and welfare?

In a divided world, can we hope to survive as a free people unless our enculturation includes the most significant generalizations, values, and processes drawn from the frontiers of knowledge?

Few local and state governments can assign qualified people to full-time curriculum research, designing, and development. The youth in all our schools must have the opportunity and encouragement to acquire the understandings, values, and competencies that are essential if free men everywhere are to survive the aggressive encroachment of both communist and fascist forces. But even if we were not threatened by to-talitarian values and institutions, we would need to provide both the content and the process that seem most likely to preserve our democratic values and help us attain the vast possibilities we see on the horizon.

Our national goals in a world setting must be examined continuously, translated into educational objectives, balanced for comprehensiveness and importance, and embodied in optional curriculum designs. Such curriculum designing requires a national and joint effort of laymen, academic scholars, and professional school personnel.

During any calendar year there are usually several national projects initiated by groups of scholars to provide schools with curriculum guides and instructional materials. Currently, national associations of mathematicians, of foreign language teachers, of physical or biological scientists, of economists or geographers are providing such leadership in their respective subject matter disciplines.

Simultaneously there are several national, regional, or state efforts initiated by associations of professional school people to improve the curriculum. However, few if any of these efforts are conceived as instrumental in pursuit of national goals, and none of these sporadic and uncoordinated efforts has a life expectancy of more than a few years.

We need a nationwide curriculum commission that is nongovernmental and has no power except the force of its rational proposals. Such a nationwide body could continuously provide the state and local lay boards and professional staffs with the best, the most comprehensive, and carefully balanced sets of educational goals related to our national purpose, together with optional curricular designs by means of which the goals could be achieved.

If we accept the basic assumptions and the logical implications of what has been said thus far, then certain suggestions are probably in order with regard to the NEA's future role in curriculum and instruction. I make the following ones with full recognition that some will challenge the assumptions and that others will question the logic of the suggestions. But our profession is a mature one and profits from discussion of differing diagnoses and presciptions.

— As the only all-encompassing educational organization in this nation, the NEA should direct a proper share of its energy (a) to engaging in curriculum research, design, and development that facilitate the national goals, and (b) to releasing the creative potential in every child and youth. Not one or the other, but both objectives should be the business of the NEA. I believe, therefore, that the NEA should immediately take steps to create a new Curriculum and Instructional Center. The NEA should seek outside funds as well as commit a substantial portion of its own resources to finance this most significant enterprise.

— The proposed NEA Curriculum and Instructional Center should exert strong, continuous leadership but should work closely with the several departments and associations of the NEA to plan jointly for the over-all curriculum research, design, and development that will contribute directly to achieving national goals.

— The new Center should exert leadership in aiding national groups of educators to undertake studies of separate aspects of the total curriculum and further provide mechanisms through which local and state school authorities ultimately might consider whether and how such separate curriculum findings might be assimilated into or replace existing programs.

— The three previous suggestions have important conditions that should be made clear in every policy statement and action of the proposed new Center. If it is agreed that decisions about the curriculum (and, to a considerable extent, decisions about instruction) are the joint responsibility of laymen, academic scholars, and professional school people, then it should follow that no one of the partners should assign to itself the directing role.

I believe therefore that this new Center would be ill-advised to take unto itself the authorship and directing role of national curriculum research, design, and development without inviting academic scholars and laymen to participate in determining purposes and ground rules.

The statesmanlike approach would be for the Center, without a hidden agenda in its pocket, to raise this question with national associations of scholars and laymen: How might all of us who are interested in the task join forces to accomplish it and how shall we severally conceive our distinctive but complementary roles?

I am not saying that the NEA should do nothing but wait for the community of scholars and the community of laymen to initiate cooperative curriculum study. The proposed new Center, representing as it would the entire teaching profession, should take the initiative and seek the cooperation of those scholarly and lay organizations that have responsibility and indispensable contributions to make to curriculum research, design, and development.

Because we school people are in the business of educating the nation's youth, it is quite natural to expect that the technical tasks of curriculum designing and instructional planning would be assigned to professional educators. But such tasks would be undertaken in terms of goals agreed upon by all who claim a stake in educational planning to promote national purposes.

— I would hope that the new NEA Curriculum and Instructional Center in joint action with laymen and scholars would be instrumental in forming some type of nationwide academy or institute or commission whose membership would reflect the best minds and spirits of these three communities.

— Such a National Commission for Curriculum Research, Design, and Development should be nongovernmental, of high national visibility, well-financed and permanently and continuously at work translating national goals into educational objectives and balanced curriculum designs. The relationship between such a National Commission and the proposed NEA Curriculum and Instructional Center should be the agenda for many work sessions among the several partners.

— The proposed Center should work closely with higher education to study the problem of preparing teachers competent in both subject matter and instructional techniques. The teacher of the twenty-first century will need much more general and special knowledge and competence than is typical of the graduates of teacher preparation programs at present.

— The Center should work with educational administrative groups and lay boards of education to enhance the provision for continuous in-service growth of teachers, who cannot depend alone on what they learned during college preparation.

These few suggestions for the future of the NEA in curriculum and instruction by no means exhaust the topic. Hopefully, they are among the considerations that should govern the early efforts of the proposed NEA Curriculum and Instructional Center.

The final reprint in this set, delivered to the 1965 meeting of the Department of Elementary School Principals of the NEA, demonstrates the evolution of my thinking on the design and implementation of a civic education curriculum. The focus of the meeting was on two approaches to the social sciences: the coordinated approach and the separate-subject approach.

Although I was disappointed that the NEA leadership did not launch the National Commission for Curriculum Research and Development proposed in 1962, the lack of action was perhaps fortunate in the long run. As the NEA turned to unionism, its public image changed and the organization probably could not have summoned the cooperation of scholars, laymen, and school people. Today the landscape seems to be ready for a fresh reconsideration of a national curriculum commission.

If in fact the notion of a national curriculum commmmission is still viable, new leadership will be needed to make the 1960 proposal for a National Curriculum Instruction Center a reality.

DESIGN FOR A
SOCIAL STUDIES PROGRAM*

8

Two members of our ten-member team have discussed the roles the social sciences, geography, and history should play in a modern social studies program. My task is to demonstrate how a multidisciplinary and coordinated social studies program can be designed for a modern school.

Our team has developed a conviction that there is great merit in providing **all** children **first** with experiences that will help them discover the structure of the relationships that are woven into the warp and woof of the culture within which they live and participate. For the beginning school grades, we advocate a multidisciplinary, a holistic, a coordinated study of people living in societies we call communities. Every one of us lives simultaneously in all of these communities: the family, the school, the neighborhood, the local, the state, the regional, the national. Beyond the borders of the national community we see multinational regional communities emerging—communities such as the Inter-American, the Atlantic, and the Pacific.

We propose to move from the smaller and more intimate communities to the larger and more inclusive communities as the child progresses through the elementary school and expands his activities geographically and culturally. We believe that by careful programming we can introduce the pupil, through inquiry, to economic, geographic, historic, social, an-

---

thropological, and political science generalizations underlying each of these enlarging communities of which he is a member.

From the beginning of our program, we deal with those component subject matters out of which the life of any community is composed. But as we study any one of these communities, we emphasize the unity of the social configuration, drawing out of context any of the separate disciplines only momentarily for a closer look. The child is helped psychologically to start his examination of human communities by studying and generalizing about total cultural patterns of intimate scale, rather than by concentrating on the separate class period or school year. This **does not** argue for the rejection or neglect of geography, history, or the several social sciences. Actually, the elementary school curriculum has been starved by failure to infuse the social studies program with sufficient generalizations and methods of inquiry from these basic disciplines. We are determined that these foundational social sciences, history, and geography must have a much greater place in the coordinated program than they have generally had in the past.

We shall now sketch in detail one design for a multidisciplinary social studies program in the elementary school and secondary school. Keep in mind that we insist there are alternative approaches to designing a social studies program. Our design is but one of such available for your study and consideration.

The model we shall demonstrate may be somewhat familiar to most of you. But be assured that much of what we have to say today goes beyond previous presentations. Any working team is bound to make additions and refinements as minds influence minds and as it profits from criticisms fed back from elementary and secondary school principals and from colleagues in the classrooms, schools, and colleges.

We begin to construct our model by asking you to imagine a preschool child standing in the middle of his vast and dimly lit world. The child is keenly aware that around him exists an exciting world of people, objects, institutions, events. These external forms and functions that bombard his senses during his waking hours threaten him fully as much as they excite him—simply because he has had little opportunity to observe these sensory inputs systematically and to relate them to himself in an organized manner. Formal schooling is the prime tool that modern man has invented to help the child discover the order and the rationale of this external world. The school curriculum must guide him in sorting out and organizing the sensory data into a mature understanding of **each** community of which he is a member.

Where shall we find the help needed for this bewildered child and his sometimes equally bewildered teacher? We believe the proper resolution can be found in a judicious use of the high priority generalizations and methods of inquiry which our colleagues in the social sciences, history, and geography have extracted and structured for us in their several disciplines.

Here (Illustration 1), represented as sunbursts over the child and his ultimate world, are the six disciplines from which our team has woven a social studies program for the elementary [and secondary] schools.

But the child's external world consists not just of events of the past; it is not history alone. The real world exists in the present. Group life is made up of physical and cultural objects that are distributed over space and have distributional relationships. So we add the sunlight of **geography** to our model.

ILLUSTRATION 1

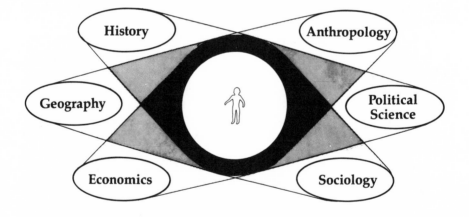

We are not content to leave the child with either a fused history-geography course or with two separate courses, one history and another geography. The man-to-man relations go far beyond these two disciplines. Ours is a multidisciplinary and coordinated approach, so our model must have light flooding from the several [social] sciences [and humanities].

Political science sheds its significant light on the processes of decision making and helps the child to see how men in communities organize to create and direct the power essential to keep a community viable.

Men strive to satisfy unlimited wants and needs with limited resources. **Economics** sheds its light on producing, exchanging, and consuming goods and services to satisfy these human wants and needs.

Men nurtured within a particular culture assimilate values, ways of thinking, and customs that profoundly affect the way individuals and groups interact. **Anthropology** helps us to understand the values, customs, and institutions of our communities and provides us with significant tools for both preserving and changing them.

And lastly, from **sociology** we gain significant generalizations and methods of inquiry into a host of man-to-man relations that we must begin to understand and learn to control. Certainly school pupils can learn elementary concepts of such sociological problems as population explosion, urban congestion, race, [diversity], automation, and human welfare.

We select **history** as one highly luminous source. We deliberately cause the bright light of historical method and cause-effect relationships generated by historical research to illuminate the dark spaces between the child and his world.

Our design for the social studies has two dimensions: a **sequence** and a **scope**. I wish to discuss now the **sequence** of themes or emphases that form one set of coordinates of our design (Illustration 2).

Each of us lives simultaneously within a set or system of enlarging but interdependent communities of men. Between the individual child and his ultimate world lie a number of communities of varying size and scale. It is the school's responsibility to help each child become aware of each community and develop competency to participate effectively in it.

At this point in our discussion of sequence, a generic definition of the term **community** is in order. **A community is any group or society of people who live in a definable geographic space; who possess sufficient historic values and customs in common to hold the society together; who face common problems; who have devised solutions (institutions, laws, customs) that are workable and somewhat unique to that community; who have developed ways of communicating; and who acknowl-**

ILLUSTRATION 2

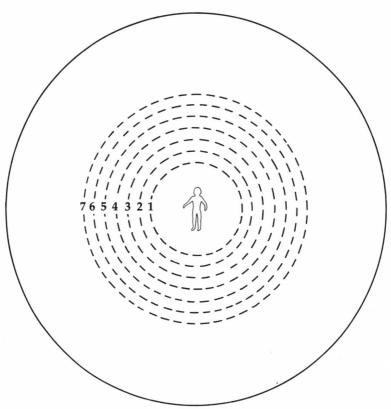

7 6 5 4 3 2 1

Expanding Communities of Men

(family through nation)

1. Family Community
2. School Community
3. Neighborhood Community
4. Local, County and
   Metropolitan Communities

5. State Community
6. Region-of-States Community
7. U.S. National Community

edge membership in the group or society. In our model we shall designate sequence.

We propose to start our multidisciplinary social studies program in the primary grades by first emphasizing the oldest, the smallest, the most intimate, and the most crucial grouping of men—the **family community**. This grouping represents the child's family—his father, mother, sisters, brothers, and other relatives who constitute a household. No other community of men equals the family in the number or in the significance of daily human relationships involving the child. The geographic arena within which this family community lives could be a palace or a slum dwelling.

The family community, however, is not the sole human group to which the child belongs. Because the family in our time is not equipped to provide all of the formal education needed, the child at five or six years of age normally becomes a member of a larger-than-family community—the school. Here the beginning school child meets many children—some of his age, but most older. His school community consists also of teachers and administrative personnel. This school community is obviously somewhat different in purpose and composition from the other communities in our sequential design, but for reasons which should be clear later, it is designated as the next larger band in this model.

Because a family cannot be completely self-sufficient, it is natural for a family to join informally with other families to form a **neighborhood community**. This next larger concentric band represents the loosely cohesive community of families who live fairly close together, who have some fairly common identifying features, and who are, by virtue of their neighborly efforts, more self-sufficient than they could be as separate families. The geographic area of the neighborhood is usually a well-recognized portion of a county or city with fairly distinctive boundaries such as a stream, a wide thoroughfare, or those set by zoning regulations. In addition to an elementary school, the neighborhood usually has churches, stores and shops, public and private recreational facilities, a branch library, and substations for mail, police, fire, and similar services. These man-made features of the neighborhood landscape extend and enrich the efforts of individual families to provide for their needs.

Once again the model expands. Since no neighborhood community is self-sufficient, neighborhoods join with neighborhoods to form **local communities** called by such terms as county, city, suburbia, and metropolis. Some of the associations that exist to serve the needs of several associated neighborhoods are the city hall, water system, market place, transportation system, newspapers, radio and TV stations, the county courthouse, medical associations, central library, the metropolitan recreation district, the law enforcement association. This complex of local communities, lying between the larger state community and the smaller neighborhood communities, is the fourth concentric band in our model of expanding communities of men. As the impact of modern science and technology mounts, as more and more neighborhoods come within the dynamic influence and boundaries of the expanding metropolis, these local communities will demand a larger proportion of our time, energy, and money.

Beyond the local communities in this model, the elementary school pupil next studies his **state community**. The geographic, historic, and political dimensions of a child's state are well defined but generally under-taught in the school curriculum. Historically, the state community came into being when the several local communities in a territory needed services which they could not provide successfully alone. The public and private institutions and organizations that operate throughout the state try to furnish the lesser communities with those services that are beyond individual capabilities of local, neighborhood, and family communities or that can be provided more effectively by the state community because of its larger resources.

In thinking about the set of interdependent communities, the citizen ordinarily moves directly from the state to the nation. This jump overlooks an increasingly crucial community that lies between—the **region of states**. The United States Bureau of the Census has recognized the growing number of common concerns of and solutions by regions. Beginning with the 1950 census, it gathered, summarized, and presented all data by four regions: South, West, North Central, and Northeast. In our model, the pupil moves from an emphasis on his state to an emphasis on his region of states, and from there to a study of the three other regions.

Note here the desirability of being flexible. For a class living in the North Central region of states, that would be the logical region to study in depth, first. For a child in my region, the West comes first. The remaining three regions could be studied in any order.

The next larger community is the **United States national community**. Within this nation today, 190 million citizens benefit from the foresight of our forefathers who wrote in the Preamble to the Constitution:

> We the people of the United States, in order to form a more perfect Union, establish justice, insure domestic tranquility, provide for the common defense, promote the general welfare, and secure the bless-

ings of liberty to ourselves and our posterity, do ordain and establish this Constitution for the United States of America.

Public and private efforts to bring about this national dream have been successful, perhaps beyond the fondest hopes of the founding fathers.

The seventh emphasis, our **national community,** completes the first subset of expanding communities. The subset, family through nation, is a highly interdependent system of interlocking [and overlapping] communities, always expanding in size and complexity. One can better understand each of the interdependent communities by studying the system. The family community in the United States can be comprehended much better by knowing the cultural complex we speak of as the national personality; one's own state can be understood much better by knowing the composite characteristics of families, neighborhoods, and local communities.

Let us now turn from the sequence dimension of our multidisciplinary social studies program to a brief discussion of the second set of coordinates of our design—**the scope**, organized into categories of basic human activities (Illustration 3). Universally, men living in groups have always carried on these activities in differing ways. There are numerous systems for cataloging or clustering these universally performed functions. The main purpose of grouping is to provide the teacher and pupil some logical and orderly way to observe and to organize their observations about the kaleidoscopic world. Whether the categories number six or sixteen is of minor importance.

Let us first identify the basic human activities of **producing, exchanging, and consuming goods and services.** Within the mind's eye there flows a rapid succession of pictures: primitive men hunting and fishing; modern men with mechanical power producing crops on the land and in the sea; men in simple cottage shops or in complex and automated factories shaping raw materials into finished goods; colorful primitive market places or the interior of a supermarket; people consuming the abundant food, clothing, and other goods available in a modern economy. These kaleidoscopic pictures are for the moment universals. They are not classified by time, by place, or by any one of the several communities of men. These further refinements of classification will be discussed later.

Now observe the remaining headings for the other eight segments. Closely allied with producing, exchanging, and consuming is the second cluster in our grid: **transporting people and goods.** The boundaries of this pie-shaped segment are **not** solid lines separating this basic human

ILLUSTRATION 3

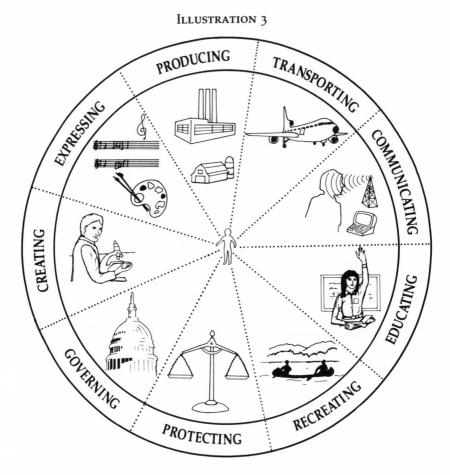

Scope

(basic human activities)

activity from the cluster on either side; these boundaries are dotted lines. Each category is partially found within several or all of the other segments. We are attempting here to focus on a cluster of activities that can be identified as distinct although not disassociated from the other clusters.

A third cluster of basic human activity we shall call **communicating fact, ideas, and feelings**. You are invited to create pictures in your mind to illustrate this activity found in every society regardless of time and place.

A fourth category is labeled **providing education**. The range of pictures comprising this activity would include such diversity as an ancient caveman teaching his offspring how to stalk and kill wild game; a child of the frontier learning from his hornbook; the modern mass education invention we call the school; a possible world learning center where programmed instruction is beamed wordwide via a network of communication satellites.

A fifth cluster is labeled **providing recreation**. All communities of men through all times have played and amused and refreshed themselves. Some societies with a luxuriant environment have placed a higher value on this basic human activity than have other societies where a barren environment forces men to work long and hard to survive, leaving little time for recreation.

A sixth cluster is labeled **protecting and conserving life, health, property, and resources**. Housing, medicine, defense, and law are illustrations of the provisions men make to satisfy the universal needs in this category.

For a seventh group of activities we use the phrase **organizing and governing**. Both public and private sectors of any community need to organize, manage, direct, administer, and govern. These activities, which we might call decision making and enforcement, range from agreements within a family to avoid conflict over the use of the telephone to the complex machinery of national governments and of the United Nations for regulating the uses of outer space.

Next we focus on a segment we call **creating new tools, technics, and institutions**. Men are forever inventing better theories and solutions, be it a better mouse trap, a new molecule, a spaceship, or a substitute for force in settling disputes.

Finally we focus on a cluster entitled **expressing aesthetic and spiritual needs**. The universal desire of men to associate with one another in pursuit of beauty, or in spiritual satisfaction, has been and continues to be one of the deepest motivations in society.

We now have a complete catalog of the basic human activities—the **scope**. It is complete to the extent that we can find a segment in the scheme into which we can easily fit any group activity that is a part of past history, contemporary life, or conceivable future. We now return to the seven [expanding] communities of men (family through nation)— the **sequence**.

So far we have detailed two dimensions of the coordinated social studies design: 1) the expanding communities **sequence** and 2) the basic

ILLUSTRATION 4

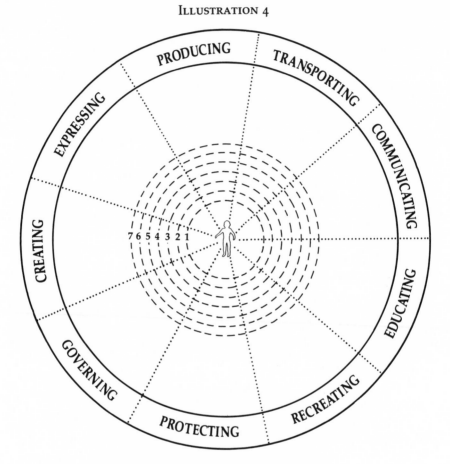

A Curriculum Design

(family through nation)

1. Family Community
2. School Community
3. Neighborhood Community
4. Local, County and
   Metropolitan Communities

5. State Community
6. Region-of-States Community
7. U.S. National Community

human activities **scope**. Now we will superimpose one of the dimensions over the other and have a composite (Illustration 4): the segments of basic human activities intersect the concentric bands of the communities of men. Each of the seven bands cuts through all nine segments. Each of the nine segments is present in all seven bands; each community of men conducts all the basic activities.

Our suggested design for the sequence of the elementary school social studies is, to this point, incomplete. We have yet to complete our particular logic of expanding communities of men by moving out beyond the national community. Modern science and technology make obsolete the once defensible notion that the nation is the outer limit of the set of expanding communities. Today, nations cannot exist as islands: some multinational values, institutions, laws, and customs are even now appearing; others wait for the time when men shall find it desirable and possible to [acknowledge and to] welcome larger-than-national communities.

Beyond the national concentric circle (number 7 in our design) we recognize three region-of-nations communities: the Inter-American community, the Atlantic community, and the Pacific community. (These three region-of-nations communities are numbers 8, 9, and 10 in Illustration 5.) Arbitrarily we choose the **United States and Inter-American community** as the eighth emphasis or band in our sequence.

This emerging community of men, with one-half billion human members, has in common more than ten thousand years of Indian history, almost five hundred years of European cultural overlay, and over one hundred years of struggle to win independence from European colonialism. These half-billion Americans are creating public and private networks of communication, production and exchange, education, and the like that knit and bind them together into a recognizable community of men that will, in the lifetime of youngsters now in our schools, become an ever increasingly important instrument for the satisfaction of human needs and aspirations.

The United States national community is a member of a second emerging region of nations: **the United States and Atlantic community**. It represents all the lands and people around the shores of the Atlantic Ocean: the Americas, Europe, the Middle East, and Africa. In the past, the Atlantic Ocean was considered a strategic defense boundary by each nation washed by its waters. In our nuclear power age, the same Atlantic Ocean is but the inner sea of an emerging Atlantic community. The outer territorial limits of such an emerging community are certainly not fixed; they are controversial and will probably always be less definite than the

ILLUSTRATION 5

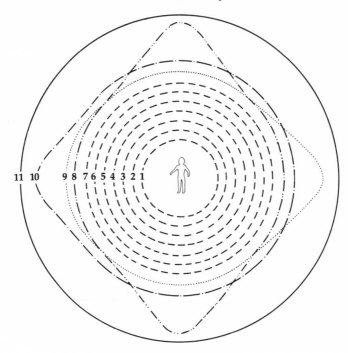

Sequence

Communities of Men
(family through world)

1. Family Community
2. School Community
3. Neighborhood Community
4. Local, County and
   Metropolitan Communities
5. State Community

6. Region-of-States Community
7. U.S. National Community
8. Inter-American Community
9. Atlantic Community
10. Pacific Community
11. The World Community

borders of a national community. But the centripetal forces pulling the outlying nations more closely into an Atlantic community are slowly but surely increasing. Predictably, they will overbalance the centrifugal forces that now operate to keep England out of the Common Market or to isolate South Africa from its Western cultural heritage.

Western culture, infused with elements of great cultures of the Middle East, permeates this vast Atlantic community arena. The democratic, industrial, and scientific revolutions have provided a cohesion that makes the former unrelated units more and more parts of a new whole. NATO, CENTO, OECD, EUROATOM, and the Afro-Anglo-American Association of Teacher Education are just a few of a long list of institutions and agencies created since World War II to serve an emerging Atlantic community. Posterity has a right to expect that our social studies program in the schools will lay the groundwork of values, understanding, and competencies required in building an Atlantic community in the decades ahead. Today's schools should not impose tomorrow's answers on school children, but schools should equip tomorrow's citizens with the skills with which they may one day fashion multinational establishments to match our soaring aspirations.

A third region of nations is emerging, named for the great Pacific Ocean that washes the shores of most of the nations of the **United States and Pacific community**. This vast arena is represented in our model by a tenth band. In this space, which covers more than two-thirds of the surface of the earth, live more than 1.8 billion people—almost two out of every three humans alive today. The Occidental Pacific and the Oriental Pacific lie far apart. Only in our time has this huge, loosely knit aggregate been regarded potentially as a region of the globe.

The possibility of a Pacific community arises out of the common frustrations and aspirations of Americans, Asians, Australians, and Oceanians. Many young nations in this emerging community are busily engaged in glorifying nationalism. At the same time, science and technology are shrinking or shattering the barriers of water, mountains, distance, language, and cultural differences. These material advances force larger-than-national concerns and will ultimately encourage mutual understanding and respect for the diverse cultures and aims of the Pacific partners. Underneath the noisy and often bitter conflicts of ideologies grow new roots of cooperation—the Pacific Science Congress, the Asian Games, the East-West Center, the Colombo Plan, and hundreds of private corporations that cross national boundaries to build economic establishments to serve an emerging Pacific community.

To begin with, we placed the child in the center of our model, and far out—the world band. We now return to the outer band. The emerging **world community**, number eleven in our sequential emphases, is not by definition a part of any larger community of men—at least not yet.

The world community is even less an actuality than the three smaller regions-of-nations communities. Conflicts divide the world into armed camps; the threat of reckless use of nuclear, bacteriological, or chemical warfare darkens the future. The Communist camp continues to subvert and threaten the neutrals and the free nations.

Yet man's ageless yearning for world peace, fraternity, and plenty gains hope anew in the successes of ecumenical conferences, increasing tourism, multilingual capability, the United Nations and its specialized agencies, the International Red Cross, the International Bank, the International Court of Justice, and scores of other public and private mechanisms created to solve problems beyond the capacity of single nations or regions of nations.

This emerging **world community** has a rich historical content of bold dreams and has made courageous attempts to bring unity to a splintered and quarreling world: Alexander the Great dreamed, acted, and came close to success. The Holy Roman Empire gave a degree of peace and prosperity to much of the Old World. The literature of most of the world's cultures contains a common theme of man's universal brotherhood. Perhaps the time is approaching when the human family will be forced to accentuate the positive and universal values of humanity as a prelude to creating world-wide conditions which will satisfy the generic definition of **community** we cited earlier. The schools of the world must prepare tomorrow's citizens to grapple successfully with problems of such global magnitude. The social studies program carries a major responsibility for this objective.

We have seen the completed sequence of eleven expanding communities of men (Illustration 5). Let us refer again to the basic human activities (Illustration 3). By superimposing the basic human activities over the set of communities of men, we create a finished social studies program design for the elementary [and secondary] schools—the basic human activities, the **scope**; the expanding communities of men, the **sequence** (Illustration 6).[1]

A detailed elaboration of all the possible teaching-learning experiences within this design is not possible. But we will illustrate how the model works, by taking you through one of the nine clusters of the basic human activities to demonstrate how it helps to focus on learning experiences in each of the eleven communities.

Let us consider, for example, that segment of basic human activities labeled **protecting and conserving health, life, property, and resources** (Illustration 7). Consider the family as it is protected by its sheltering house. You can think of scores of other ways Mary's family or John's family protects and conserves, to round out the possibilities for learning experiences found within the intersection of this "protecting" segment and this "family" band.

ILLUSTRATION 6

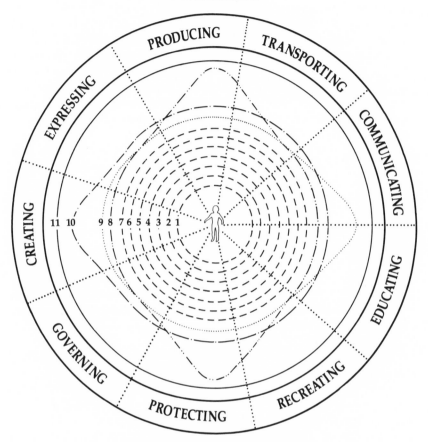

A Curriculum Design
(family through world)

The next larger community, the **school**, where it intersects with **protecting and conserving health, life, property, and resources**, offers different types of protecting activities.

Again expand the size of the community. For the **neighborhood**, fire protection is just one of the many ways a community of this scale protects life and property. Obviously each family could not afford to maintain modern fire protection equipment; the solution is found in the ap-

ILLUSTRATION 7

Communities Protect

7 The Nation Protects

8 The Inter-American
   Community Protects

9 The Atlantic Community
   Protects

10 The Pacific Community
    Protects

11 The World Community
    Protects

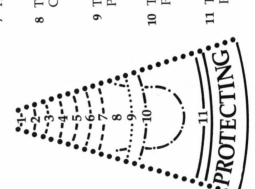

PROTECTING

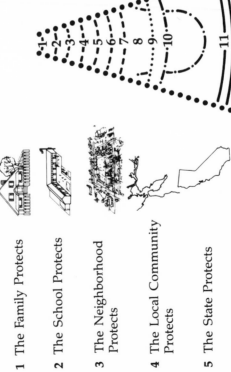

1 The Family Protects

2 The School Protects

3 The Neighborhood
   Protects

4 The Local Community
   Protects

5 The State Protects

6 The Region-of-States
   Protects

propriate scale community—the neighborhood or the local community. You have probably already formed a dozen pictures in your mind of other ways that a neighborhood protects and conserves through such means as police, clinics, or rules regarding bicycles.

Once more, increase the community size and note that a medical society in the **local communities** is one illustration of protecting and conserving.

Increase the community size again. The **state community** could be represented by any one of many ways a state concerns itself with protecting and conserving.

Again enlarge the community. Note that a **region-of-states community** could build a great dam to conserve its water and soil resources. Conservation in a river basin that cuts through several states is more properly the responsibility of the region of states than it is of any individual state.

We come next to the **national community**. Consider the readiness of our national defenses to ward off possible air attacks. Here is a problem of such size and complexity that it is properly placed by the lesser communities into the hands of the larger and inclusive national community.

Moving beyond the national community to an emerging **United States and Inter-American community**, let us consider the Organization of American States (OAS), one of the newer developments of a multinational nature to protect this hemisphere against aggression and to conserve and use the vast resources of the Americas.

Another region-of-nations community, an emerging **United States and Atlantic community**, is next shown as protecting some of its member nations by a unique alliance called NATO, the North Atlantic Treaty Organization. This Atlantic community has already developed scores of scientific and social technologies that contribute to the health and wealth of the peoples of this arena.

In the third multinational complex, an emerging **United States and Pacific community**, the SEATO military alliance, the South-East Asia Treaty Organization, exists to protect the lives and property of certain member nations. Another example is the Pacific Science Congress which is researching to conquer disease and malnutrition in this vast arena.

We conclude this series of quick glimpses into possible teaching-learning experiences of protecting and conserving with the World Health Organization, the purpose of which is to make the entire earth a more healthful place in which to dwell.

We could have used any of the other basic human activities to demonstrate the infinite possibilities of this design.

Now we will demonstrate rapidly the linkage of all the nine basic human activities of our scope as they are used to guide the study of one of the expanding communities, **the nation** (Illustration 8). Think first of **producing, exchanging, and consuming goods and services**.

Now observe the section of the national community band entitled **transporting**. Recall a map of the United States showing the interstate highway system. Air, water, or rail networks also illustrate the national effort to supply transportation services.

ILLUSTRATION 8

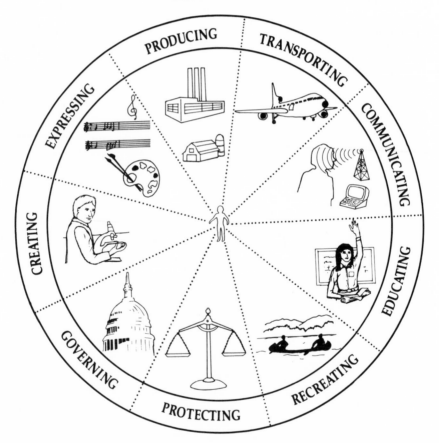

The Nation

Examine briefly the intersection of the national community and the problems of **communicating** and imagine the confusion if the federal postal service were carried on by 50 competing state systems! Nation-wide telephone, radio, and TV networks, the press wireservices, and many other activities can be grouped within a study of these national efforts in communicating.

Again we shift focus. This time consider the national effort to **provide education**, both as an item of personal consumption and as a national investment.

Next consider **providing recreation**. Perhaps the networks of national parks best illustrate this type of national effort.

Next comes **protecting and conserving**. The activities of [national] forest rangers come within this category.

For the intersection of **organizing and governing** in the national community band, political science and business administration would furnish us with many good elementary and advanced topics.

The national community **creates new tools, technics, and institutions**. This is illustrated by Telstar or by a nuclear reactor, a national cancer research laboratory, or Project English.

We finally complete our study of the national community band by focusing our attention on **expressing and satisfying aesthetic and religious needs**. An infinite variety of national activities can be studied within this focus.

This brief discussion of the national community illustrates how our team has used the design as a frame on which to fasten the generalizations, methods of inquiry, and structures of history, geography, and the social sciences (Illustration 9). The United States national community exists in physical space. Knowledge of the distribution of physical and cultural features over the nation is indispensable to an understanding of our national problems and our successes.

The light of **geography** shining on the clusters of basic human activities helps to explain why the distributions are as they are and how transportation, production, consumption, protection, recreation, and so on are interrelated and are also influenced by the earth's physical features.

But the national community exists in time as well as in space. The sunburst of **history** highlights another indispensable structuring of knowledge which the pupil must master. How have the available tools, mechanical power, and social technologies affected the geography and changed the character of the ways each of the basic human activities has been carried on in this national arena from the time of the first Indians right up through the present? And what may we speculate about our

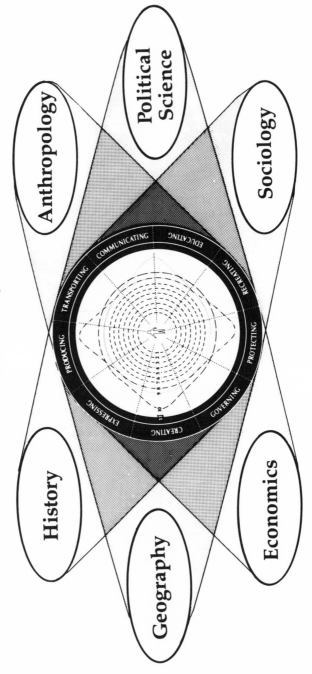

ILLUSTRATION 9

creative efforts to provide new solutions for tomorrow? Clearly, history gives us tools by which we can reconstruct the long story of development of a community over time, and even project the future in broad strokes. History and geography are essential and related components for the study of every community of whatever scale in a modern, multidisciplinary social studies program.

But we cannot end our floodlighting of the national community with light from only geography and history. A community must organize to make and carry out decisions on behalf of the community. Light from **political science** shows us how the national efforts of both government and private sectors solve the problems of organizing and governing and helps us to understand the rationale behind the diverse solutions.

It is clear that many of the categories of basic human activities of our design are aspects of the science of **economics**. So the sunburst of this discipline becomes an important component of our coordinated social studies program. Such national activities as producing, exchanging, consuming, transporting, or communicating are understood and mastered better as one gains knowledge and skill in the elements of economics. But again we raise a basic question: Can one tell where economics ends and political science begins? Where can geography and history be found in pure form unrelated to economics and political science? We see as the reasonable solution to the social studies program of the schools a holistic design that uses all the scholarship we can obtain to throw its coordinated light on the study of each expanding community in [the sequence of] our design.

Any study of the national community is incomplete without the structured generalizations and methods of inquiry of **anthropology** and **sociology**. Both of these social sciences are increasingly important to a minimal understanding of any community by a modern man.

This design provides a way of organizing the generalizations, methods of inquiry, and structures of history, geography, and the social sciences. It is a design that applies not only to a study of the national community, which we have used as an illustration, but also to a study of all the other communities of men (Illustration 9).

The logic of this coordinated social studies design suggests that the pupil study each larger community in sequence. In the kindergarten and first grade, the child might begin his study of the system with emphasis on his own family and on his own school. As he studies each of these communities, he learns what phases of life are properly the concern of himself as a member of these small intimate groups. He also learns that families need to join together to provide for the satisfaction of many needs through neighborhood apparatuses. Consequently, the child moves naturally to the third emphasis in the sequential design—his neighborhood community which provides services not available to families or to schools working alone.

This particular social studies design may assign the study of the child's neighborhood to the second grade. However, the community to be emphasized in any particular grade is relatively unimportant. Following the sequence from the lesser community to the next larger is the governing principle.

The sequence typically followed in schools adopting such a structure is to complete the sequence of eleven community emphases by the end of grade 6. It is equally defensible to stretch out the time for covering the eleven communities over seven—or even eight—grades. Any design must be flexible enough to accommodate differences in pupil ability or differences in the expectations of patrons and professionals at the local or state community levels.

Another principle essential to this particular design: The pupils constantly move inward and outward among the several communities. As each community is studied, children should be helped to see that many problems they examine thrust them inevitably into larger communities for solution. There is always a forward look, anticipating the several communities that lie ahead for deeper study in later grades. At the same time, there must always be a review and a deepening of insights concerning the smaller communities previously emphasized. A child is not through studying the **family** at the end of the first grade. In each expanding community, provision is made for a fuller study of the smaller communities previously emphasized and of the larger ones to follow.

There is still another characteristic of this design. When youngsters are studying their own state, for instance, they will naturally compare and contrast other states. To the extent that there are meaningful bridges to a state or its equivalent in Mexico, Japan, or Switzerland, these exciting and enriching experiences should be incorporated as part of the work. But the teacher **must** be responsible for bringing youngsters back from these useful side excursions to the major arena, which in this case is the state community.

Many of us believe it is desirable to plan the design of the coordinated social studies program as a kindergarten through grade 12 continuum. Assuming that some such strategy of "studying how men carry on the basic human activities in a system of expanding communities of men" has been rounded out in the elementary school, we contend that adolescents in the secondary school would be more ready to pursue profitably a program of separate study of each of the several social science disciplines, geography, and history. The final proof of such a contention has yet to be fully documented; but a multidisciplinary and coordinated design for the elementary school social studies program makes sense to us. We hope it does to many of you, your teachers, your pupils, and your communities. But the major task confronting us is to examine all design proposals critically and then lead our staffs in a continuous search for better content, structure, and methods in the social studies program.

NOTE

1. These proposals are just as applicable to social studies programs in today's middle schools—Paul R. Hanna.

Concluding Remarks

What are the chances in the 1980s and 1990s that scholars, laymen, and educators could, in the present climate, work together to form a national commission to identify the highest priority goals of schooling and to create alternative scope-and-sequence matrices for curriculum and instruction? The chances of a successful joint effort currently seem to me to be very promising.

The **scholarly** community demonstrated its interest in engaging in such an effort in the recent announcement of the American Association for the Advancement of Science of *Project 2061, Education for a Changing Future*. In Phase I of the project, mathematicians, scientists, and technologists will select the vital content and theories of science; that is, they will attempt to "identify the core of scientific knowledge that should be included in the education of all young Americans." In Phase II, *Formulation*, the project "will take a new look at the educational approaches necessary to achieve the goals identified in Phase I." In Phase III, *Implementation*, the project "will encourage the adoption of these new goals and approaches by the nation's many and varied school systems, and provide practical guidance."

The **lay community** in 1985 published a brochure entitled *Investing in Our Children: Business and the Public Schools*. This publication was produced by the Research and Policy Committee of the Committee for Economic Development (CED). The committee stated that it is "keenly aware of education's role in producing informed and productive citizens . . .

The Mission and purpose of our public schools go far beyond the preparation of young people for employment. Our schools should prepare our children to exercise the rights and obligations of citizenship." Thus have laymen indicated an interest in school curriculum and instruction.

Another excellent study was produced in 1986 by the Carnegie Forum on Education and the Economy. This statement was written by a combination of scholars, educators, and laymen and entitled *A Nation Prepared: Teachers for the 21st Century.* This group centers its research and proposals on the selection and preparation of teachers for our schools. Members state that "America's ability to compete in world markets is eroding. The productivity growth of our competitors outdistances our own. The capacity of our economy to provide a high standard of living for all our people is increasingly in doubt . . . As in past economic and social crises, Americans turn to education. They rightly demand an improved supply of young people with the knowledge, the spirit, the stamina, and the skills to make the nation once again fully competitive— in industry, in commerce, in social justice and progress, and, not least, in the ideas that safeguard a free society."

To complete the list of groups who should join in efforts to create a national commission for curriculum research and development, we find two reports from leaders who are essentially **educators**: the 1983 report of the Education Commission of the States, *Action for Excellence*; and the 1983 publication by the National Commission on Excellence in Education, *A Nation at Risk.* Both groups recommended that we identify the high-priority values of our society, the most basic concepts and generalizations of useful knowledge, and the skills essential to our survival and progress. Relatively little effort was made to list these values, understandings, and skills that should be the educational outcomes of attending school in America. But these reports seem to argue that such curriculum and instruction guides are essential if our schools are to be effective.

Recommended Reading

1. *A Nation at Risk*, National Commission on Excellence in Education, 1983.
2. *Action for Excellence, Task Force on Education and the Economy*, Education Commission of the States, 1983.
3. *Investing in Our Children: Business and Our Schools*, Research and Policy Committee of the Committee for Economic Development, 1985.
4. *A Nation Prepared: Teachers for the 21st Century*, Carnegie Forum on Education and the Economy, Carnegie Corporation of New York, 1986.
5. *Project 2061: Education for a Changing Future*, American Association for the Advancement of Science, 1986–87.
6. *The Teaching of Values in Higher Education*, Woodrow Wilson International Center for Scholars, 1986.